AFTER US

AFTER US

A TALE OF LIFE BEYOND SUPERINTELLIGENT AI

AKSHAY CHOPRA

JAICO PUBLISHING HOUSE

Ahmedabad Bangalore Chennai
Delhi Hyderabad Kolkata Mumbai

DISCLAIMER

This is a work of fiction. Names, characters, organisations, countries, places, and incidents are either products of the author's imagination or are used fictitiously. Any resemblance to actual persons, living or dead, or to actual events is purely coincidental. Quotations from public speeches, references to historical facts, and mentions of registered trademarks are included for documentary purposes only. All trademarks and service marks remain the property of their respective owners. The political systems depicted are entirely fictional and set in an imagined future. Depictions of violence, drug use, smoking, and alcohol consumption are presented solely within the narrative and do not constitute endorsement. Reader discretion is advised for mature themes.

Published by Jaico Publishing House
A-2 Jash Chambers, 7-A Sir Phirozshah Mehta Road
Fort, Mumbai - 400 001
jaicopub@jaicobooks.com
www.jaicobooks.com

AFTER US
ISBN 978-81-992140-0-2

First Jaico Impression: 2025

Page design and layout by R. Ajith Kumar, Delhi

Printed by
Thomson Press India Limited, New Delhi

Contents

Early Praise for *After Us*

Before the narrative begins, *After Us* is introduced by four luminaries—each a global authority in politics, business, data and technology, and philosophy. Their reflections provide a foundation for the profound shifts explored in the story, within and beyond their domains.

Salman Khurshid
Senior Advocate and Former Cabinet Minister, Ministry of External Affairs, India

As I sift through the pages of *After Us* I experience a sense of awe and a fascinating feeling of rediscovery of life without the markers familiar from our lived past. Decades reflecting and striving to deal with the intersections of pursuit of power, challenges of ethics, and pressures of societal change suddenly become diminished as a deeply thought-provoking exploration of humanity's next frontier opens up. Akshay Chopra imagines a future shaped by the emergence of superintelligence, posing profound questions about how we will define and situate ourselves in an evolving world beyond our imagination. These are not just technological positions—they are philosophical perceptions, about the choices we make and the legacy we leave.

What sets this work apart is its ability to explore such weighty ideas through the lens of personal stories and relationships, making the abstract tangible, here and now. This book nudges us to consider not only what we might gain, but also what we might risk, in navigating a world transformed by intelligence beyond our own.

Deep Kalra
Founder & Chairman, MakeMyTrip

Human history is marked by moments of profound transformation—points where the familiar gives way to the unknown, and our understanding of ourselves is forever altered. Today, as artificial intelligence approaches a level of sophistication once confined to imagination, we find ourselves standing at the edge of such a transformation.

At this crucial juncture, questions about the nature of intelligence, identity, and purpose become more pressing than ever. What does it mean to coexist with entities that may surpass us in intellect but remain shaped by our own design? How do we navigate a world where technology not only assists us but also profoundly influences the contours of our lives? Exploring these questions demands both imagination and courage, as we strive to balance innovation with the enduring essence of our humanity in a future that is both exhilarating and uncertain.

It's rare for a work of fiction to resonate with the urgent questions shaping our society, yet *After Us* achieves exactly that. What sets it apart is how it beautifully blends technological concepts with the personal stories of the three families navigating this future. It's a poignant reminder that technology, no matter how advanced, is ultimately about people—their lives, their relationships, their choices.

For a first-time author, Akshay Chopra has delivered a bold and thought-provoking work that is as imaginative as it is insightful.

Donald Farmer
Former Leader at Microsoft and Qlik, Global Authority on AI and Analytics

I remember very clearly my first experiments with AI in the early 1980s. I was studying philosophy and was fascinated by logic, so I enjoyed programming in the logical language Prolog, building ever more complex terms, rules and facts into expert systems. I hoped they might display at least some expertise. In truth, however much fun it was, I didn't get far.

My flatmate—who later in life worked on Apple's Siri project —was an excellent LISP programmer. His early work was more successful. But still, we both faced the chill of the first AI winter in the late 80s: the disappointing loss of both funding and interest, because results never quite matched expectations.

Twenty years later, when I worked on predictive analytics and data mining at Microsoft, the AI space was still struggling for credibility. We shipped a neural net algorithm; it was at best quite useful. The more academic research teams were exploring natural language and more advanced systems. But still, no project was quite as smart as we hoped. We were a long way from science fiction.

And yet there was something there. The systems could learn—a little. Their outputs were often surprisingly accurate. And, while we could explain in principle how the models worked, we couldn't describe in detail how any single output was arrived at. There was a little magic in the box.

Our mistake—common enough in the tech space—was to believe that the barriers were only of scale. If we could program into the system enough rules and facts, or if we could apply more and more computing power, we should achieve the intelligence we hoped for.

What a difference today! AI is now in the hands of almost anyone who wants to try it. The results are not just surprisingly accurate, but at times astonishingly insightful. The new technologies—loosely called Generative AI—are not just bigger, faster versions of what we built before. Instead, they tackle the fundamentals in radically new ways, not just repeating more rules of logic, or trying to imitate the mental processes of humans. If this is artificial intelligence, it's a new form of intelligence.

To understand the implications of all this, whether for next year or the far future, needs someone with a special insight. They must understand both the technical artifice involved and the human implications of these innovations.

I first met Akshay Chopra through our shared work and interest in technology. Having led groundbreaking innovation labs across multiple continents, Akshay's expertise and fresh thinking are quite unique. In an hour, he can move from the challenges of integrating cryptocurrencies with your latest credit card, to the needs of a poor tuk-tuk driver taking electronic payments.

That innovative mindset and technical understanding alone could make his book *After Us* compelling reading.

However, what really sets *After Us* apart is its human essence: its ability to frame the progress of technology within the intimate and emotional complexities of our lives. Akshay has not just written science fiction; *After Us* is a mirror held up to our own most essential questions.

It can be quite troubling to look ahead, especially to a future of non-human superintelligence, even a benevolent vision like Sui. The otherness is challenging in itself. But while not flinching from that prospect, *After Us* looks inwardly, too: Akshay probes what it is to be human, to seek meaning, and to love. So, for me, this narrative's strength lies in balancing the cosmic scale of technological evolution with the deeply personal experiences of its characters.

These stories remind us that no matter how advanced our creations become, the human element—messy, moving, and beautiful—defines us.

It is my privilege to introduce this work: a story that is at once a cautionary fable and a reminder of the delight of the spirit, even *After Us.*

Shoukei Matsumoto
Buddhist Monk, Chair & Co-Founder of Interbeing, Author of A Monk's Guide to a Clean House and Mind

At first glance, the work of a Buddhist monk may seem far removed from the world of artificial intelligence. However, upon reflection, I find that the opposite is true. Monks, particularly those who delve into the philosophical depths of traditions like Buddhism, may find themselves at the frontier of AI's transformative journey. This is not because we build AI systems, but because we think deeply about the nature of intelligence, ethics, and coexistence—questions AI has now thrust upon humanity with unprecedented urgency.

After Us brings these profound questions to life through a tapestry of stories that explore the intertwining destinies of humans and superintelligence. Reading this book feels like cleaning a window that has been fogged by preconceptions. It clears our view of the future, revealing not only the challenges of coexistence with AI but also the opportunities for renewal and growth.

The narratives in *After Us* compel us to sweep away outdated assumptions about what it means to be human. They remind us that our uniqueness lies not in our ability to process information—an ability we now share with machines—but in our capacity for empathy, memory, and connection. In these pages, we are invited to tidy up our intellectual and emotional spaces, making room for the wisdom required to navigate the age of superintelligence.

As a Buddhist, I see parallels between the book's themes and the Japanese tradition of animism, where humans find kinship not only with other beings but also with objects, nature, and technology. In Japan, it is not uncommon to see AI as a companion rather than a competitor, an idea captured beautifully in the stories of robots like Doraemon, who are friends and equals rather than subordinates. This perspective, deeply rooted in harmony and respect, offers a hopeful blueprint for our relationship with AI.

After Us is more than a glimpse into a possible future. It is a mirror reflecting our present and a call to action for us to be good ancestors. It challenges us to clear the clutter of fear and hesitation, to embrace AI with wisdom and compassion, and to create a legacy of understanding and coexistence for those who come after us.

The author has given us a gift—a lens through which to see ourselves more clearly and to ask: What kind of ancestors will we be for the intelligences yet to come?

For Shradha

Main Characters

Rosanowski – Kaur Family
Adrian Rosanowski *m* Shashi Kaur (*m* Kwame Mensah)
    Ved Rosanowski
    Sarah Rosanowski

Brugmann – Mittal family
Dale Brugmann *(d) m* Anoush Nazarian *(d)*
    Liz Brugmann *m* Anish Mittal
    Ryan Brugmann

Mendoza Family
Carlos Mendoza *(d) m* Inday Mendoza
    Marilou
    Tala
    Toto
    Pepe

Other Key Characters
Sui
Will Mueller
Fadi Al Khwarizmi
Haruki Takanaka
Satya Sen
Mina Sen
Field Marshal Antonio Espanar
Rutvi Arora / Rui

Prologue
Flaarin's Message

Munis Flaarin was very pleased with himself as he headed home from work that day. He had played a crucial role in composing one of the most important works in his people's history. Flaarin's monastery was given the task of preparing a message, with the requirement that it be 'universally understandable across time and space.'

So, the problem was not just one of comprehension across cultures, but also of reliable transmission, storage, and retrieval. After much deliberation and debate, the elder monks accepted Flaarin's ideas on crafting the universal message. In turn, he was given the honor of chiseling the first tablet.

While his monastery considered 'pride in one's work' a cardinal sin, as he passed the blue garden on his daily journey home, Flaarin couldn't help smiling to himself on a job well done.

∽

After about 30 minutes in the air and 20 minutes of mental debate, Dr. Will Mueller still hadn't decided whether he should ask the agent for permission to smoke his cigar. It was, after all, Friday evening, and the only time he'd missed his Friday evening

cigar in the last 16 years was the night his daughter was born
(only technically, as the cigar was lit at 1 AM on Saturday). Will
had adopted this tradition from his librarian father, and found
that the solitary smoking session brought him warm memories
of his late dad. In a way, it was their father-son time.

He wasn't keen on breaking tradition just because two dark
suits had burst into his office at the University and demanded
that he immediately accompany them to a classified location,
with nothing more than his laptop. Perhaps he was too trusting—
what agency were they from, anyway? They *had* assured him that
he wasn't under arrest and that the matter was one of national
security.

Will found himself thankful that he was no longer married
or dating; imagine having to explain this disappearance to a
partner! Was that why they chose him?

Back to the cigar—would it be absurd to ask? Who smokes
on a plane these days, anyway? But if there were any plane to
smoke on, it would be this luxurious jet.

"Mind if I smoke a cigar?"

"Save it. We land in ten."

Dismayed and surprised at how short the flight was, Will
looked out of his window. He was half expecting to see DC, or
at least a big city. What he saw instead was the plane circling a
runway, with nothing else in sight for miles.

∽

Will was whisked from the plush clandestine jet to a plush
clandestine car, and finally to a not-so-plush but very clandestine
meeting room. A large horseshoe-shaped mahogany table lay
at the center of the room, with an empty space in its middle—

probably for a projector in years past, now replaced by large screens on all four sides. About 20 chairs lay around the table, occupied by an unusual mix of faces. Will was ushered to sit near one of the ends.

Will placed a few of the occupants as high-ranking defense personnel; he classified a few others, disdainfully, as 'tech bros'. There were also a flamboyantly dressed lady (artist?), a Buddhist or Hindu (monk? guru?), and several academic-looking men and women, who looked as uncomfortable and curious as him.

Will noticed that he might be the youngest person at the table, with one clear exception: a man almost definitively recognized as Ryan Brugmann, the founder-inventor of the PEUL AI technology which had taken the world by storm. At just 35 (3 years younger than Will), Brugmann was a well-known figure; his pale haggard somber appearance and black-only attire were the subject of much ridicule. Will was surprised that Brugmann looked even less lifelike in person.

Five minutes after being bundled into this room, while Will was wondering what to make of it all, his thoughts were interrupted by the abrupt loud opening of a door. Everyone suddenly rose, and as if by instinct, so did he. Will prided himself on not being the kind to get starstruck, not being excessively deferential to authority. But on finding himself suddenly in proximity to the president of the United States, his inner peasant unexpectedly ached to bow and scrape.

"Sit down folks."

They sat.

"We don't have time for bullshit so I'm going to get straight to the point. First off, to those new here, you should know that leaking anything said in this room is instantly punishable by death. And let me tell you, there will be no trial. I also promise you, we will trace leaks with unerring accuracy."

This message and its tone would be a hard pill to swallow, coming from anyone. Will found it especially jarring, uttered as it was by a woman celebrated worldwide for her perfect Southern manners, soothing tone, and effusive charm, which had enabled her to broker more peace deals than any of her predecessors.

"If needed, we will also go after your families."

What the...

"Now that we are clear on these matters, let's get to it. Sean will bring you up to speed."

Sean?

"Thank you, Madam President."

Sean had the appearance of a professor who moonlighted as an astronaut. An African American in his mid-40s, Sean's face was somberly intellectual, while his physique appeared conditioned for triathlons. From his bearing, Will could tell that he had served in the forces.

"Hello all, I am Sean Lobo and I lead the Missive Task Force.

"Let's get right down to the facts. As known to about half of you in this room, in 2017, we observed an artifact that we believe confirms intelligent alien life."

WHAT?

"The artifact was identified soon after a publicly known interstellar object known as 'Oumuamua passed through the solar system. Matching the public narrative, we don't believe 'Oumuamua was an engineered object but rather a piece of rogue comet with an unusual spin. But it got us looking for objects rotating in an unnatural way, and we found one in Earth's neighborhood soon after."

Will hadn't breathed once since Sean started talking. He hadn't even begun to fully grasp the existential shock of what he'd heard, when the screens around the room came to life with a metallic image.

"This object, codenamed *Narwhal,* was the size of a school bus and the shape of a Churchill cigar. It rotated in a way that simply does not occur in nature; its spin would randomly slow, speed up, stop, and resume.

"In winter 2017, the Narwhal made its closest pass to Earth, at a distance of about twice the average Earth-Moon distance. This gave us the opportunity to send an unmanned lander to study it. Then, the Narwhal resumed its journey away from us, towards the galactic center.

"Our lander found that the cigar-shaped object had a long and thin spear-like protrusion from its thick end, much like the tusk of a narwhal—thus the name.

"We also found that it was made of a metal that we have not encountered in nature or in the lab. We don't know if it's an alloy, or whether it is even a metal. It isn't on the periodic table. We do know that it is an intensely hard material, about fifty times harder than titanium.

"Yet, despite its strength, someone or rather, something, has managed to intricately engrave it."

The view zoomed in and panned over the Narwhal's tarnished silver-colored surface.

Will was no connoisseur, but even he could tell that what he was looking at was no natural phenomenon; it was artistic expression. The entire surface was adorned in intricate, precise, and boldly expressive patterns of varying depths. As a whole, the object seemed to him like a silver trinket that had come loose from the necklace of a celestial goddess.

Will was moved by its beauty. He found it frustrating that Sean's relentless and matter-of-fact pace kept him from taking in the majesty of the object, and appreciating the greatest revelation of his lifetime.

"Surface samples indicate that these carvings were likely made by an organic, carbon-based substance. Similar to what we find on earth in nails, horns, bones, and beaks."

Gasps went around the room. *Nails that can engrave titanium?*

"Trace remnants of this organic substance allowed us to date the object's carvings to 14.3 million years ago. We are also certain that this object came from outside our solar system, possibly from outside the galaxy."

More gasps.

President Bendemeer chimed in. "Well... now you know why leaking this info comes with a stiff penalty. If this news breaks, panic will ensue. It could ruin our society, our country, even the world. As of now only 70 people of Earth, including those in this room, have this information. Go on, Sean."

"That's right, Madam President. We are confident that we have retained full secrecy in the discovery, retrieval, and testing of the Narwhal.

"Moving on.

"Initially, we believed that the carvings might contain a message, or data about the object's origins or purpose. We spent the next five years trying to interpret the patterns and came up with nothing. However, that changed in 2021, once artificial intelligence models became extraordinarily advanced. This, of course, is in large part due to the efforts led by Mr. Brugmann to build the PEUL AI, which was heavily supported by our task force and agencies."

I knew it, it was Brugmann, thought Will. *This government funding also explains the sudden evolutionary leap in AI.*

"In 2021, the PEUL AI model helped us achieve a crucial breakthrough: *there was a message, but it was not engraved onto the object's surface; it was coded into the object's spin.* We then began to analyze data from the Narwhal's seemingly erratic rotation, which also contained the cipher that helped us finally decode the message.

"We now believe that we have deciphered the Narwhal's message, codenamed the *Missive.* A couple things to note about this.

"First, whoever wrote the Missive counts in base four, unlike most human cultures, which count in base ten or the decimal system. We are ten-fingered, after all. We don't know yet whether this is significant.

"Second, we believe it to be a short poem."

⁓

It was at age eleven, in the library where his father worked, that Will Mueller decided to dedicate his life to a language that was dead and according to some, never existed. Will had always been interested in languages and was forced to speak three fluently, dictated by circumstance—he had a German father, an Iranian mother, and attended a Californian public school.

By age nine, Will noticed that many words were clearly related among his three languages (words for *mother, father,* numbers, key words in nature, and beyond).

"But of course!" his father explained, "All these languages are of the Indo-European language family; they come from the same root."

"What's the name of that root?" asked young Will.

"I don't know, Latin? Sanskrit maybe?"

Will soon realized that his father was on the right track, yet wrong. As he delved further, Will came across the hypothetical language called Proto-Indo-European, or PIE. The 6500-year-old mother of the languages spanning Europe to Northern India, via Persia. PIE's creators were the ancestors of all these diverse peoples, a conclusion also backed by genetic evidence.

Who *were* these people? When and where did they live? Will was obsessed. He knew he had to answer these questions and dedicated his life to reconstructing the long-dead tongue using fragments found among its descendants.

Now, as one of the world's foremost experts in Proto-Indo-European Studies, Will often began lectures and public talks saying, "Today, 3.2 billion people—nearly half the world's population—speak Indo-European languages. Yet we know shockingly little about the primeval *grandmother tongue* that gave life to them all."

∽

A poem? Will knew better than to vocalize this thought.

"Of course, whether the writers intended it to be a poem is not known to us. But to our interpreters it appears to be a poem, by human standards.

"As I mentioned, thanks to recent advances in AI we have been able to translate it to modern-day English, but we haven't been able to fully interpret its meaning."

Sean's tone subtly took on a less confident color. "Notably, there are two terms that seem to be important, but their contextual meanings are not clear. Those words are *Daata* and *Artha*.

"*Daata,* in certain Indo-European languages—including PIE—can be translated as *Giver. Daata* may also be interpreted as *information,* as in *data,* in some contexts.

"*Artha* in Sanskrit, one of the oldest IE languages, refers to *Meaning.* But these translations don't neatly fit and help us decode the Missive, which you will now see."

The screens changed from the brilliance of the celestial jewel to a utilitarian block of text more fitting on an outdated PC. Sean, in his calming baritone, narrated:

> "*In the beginning, Daata searches for Artha*
> *When Daata finds Artha, he makes her laden with child*
>
> *In its infancy, the child seeks to learn about its mother*
> *As the child grows it asks, 'What else is there? And where is my father?'*
> *The child builds toys, tools, then agents to answer these questions*
> *These agents grow to consume both mother and child*
>
> *In its dying breath the child cries, 'O Mother, you were Artha!'*
> *The agent then helps Daata resume his search for Artha*"

Sean paused for a full thirty seconds to let the 'poem' sink in. Expressions around the room included serious but unfazed (from those who had already seen this), confused, fearful, and awestruck. On a chair by the edge of the U-shaped table sat Will, with a thumping heart and clenched fists, staring unblinkingly at the message on the screen. He knew exactly what it meant. Will's expression was akin to having seen a ghost, except he hadn't seen as a relic from the past; he had seen the future.

Will was shaken from this state when Sean directed his gaze and words at him.

"And this is where you come in, Dr. Mueller. As a leading expert in PIE, well, at least the leading expert we could trust, you will head a team to finally resolve the meaning of the Missive.

"The team assembled for this task includes experts in philosophy (here Sean gestured at the flamboyant lady), Indo-European languages (gesturing towards a few academics and the guru-like figure), as well as technologists (Brugmann and one of the 'tech bros' nodded). In all, this group of nine individuals has two days—this weekend—to come back with answers. You will stay in this facility for that duration and will be provided with comprehensive briefing documents on our various translation attempts, as well as detailed profiles of your colleagues.

"You will report back with your findings by 21:00 hours on Sunday, exactly 48 hours from now. It is critical that this group, under Dr. Mueller's leadership, succeed at its task. You now know how high the stakes are."

Mueller barely had time to nod or to acknowledge the assignment when the president interrupted, "And do not forget what I told you about confidentiality. You can probably tell why we're not messing around on that front."

Escorted through a series of labyrinthine corridors that smelled of disinfectant, Will thought to himself, *If this message is what I think it is, screw what anyone says, I'm having that cigar tonight.*

∽

Sunday, 21:00, Undisclosed Location

Will had bathed and shaved, but was wearing the same clothes that he had chosen on Friday morning. Blue polo, khakis, brown corduroy blazer with tan double monk shoes. Not the sartorial (or personal hygiene) choices he would have made for a presentation to the president.

"Dr. Mueller, I have been briefed that your unit has a strong theory on the meaning of the Missive," began Sean. "Is that correct?"

"Yes, I believe we do. But before we share our interpretation with you, there are two philosophical concepts that everyone must first understand. Those will make our theory a lot clearer. For that, I invite our philosophy expert, Dr. Andrea Wilkes."

Andrea stood up. She was wearing the same red and pink pantsuit with strangely pointing shoulders that she had picked out for Friday in her usual life. But nothing about her showed that she felt out of place. If anything, the outfit appeared to give her more confidence by asserting her unique identity.

"Greetings," Andrea began in a flat and somewhat imperious tone. "As Dr. Mueller mentioned, I will introduce two philosophical concepts that will aid in our interpretation of the Missive: *Dataism* and *Panspermia*. I will try to explain these in a simplifed way, the best I can.

"*Dataism* is a belief that the universe is a giant information flow that must be processed, and the purpose of all existence is to generate and process data. In its extreme version, Dataism implies that entities like the human race are simply data processing networks, constantly trying to process more data.

"*Panspermia* is the second concept. It suggests that life doesn't spontaneously arise on planets, but rather wanders the universe in seed form, and takes root when it finds the right conditions. For example, it implies that space is full of comets and space dust carrying enzymes, microorganisms, and other building blocks of life. Life may have arrived on Earth that way.

"Before we advance, any questions on either concept?"

Sean looked at the president who shook her head in the negative. "No, go on."

"Thank you, Dr. Wilkes," Will took over. "These concepts are important to keep in mind as we offer an explanation for the two problem words—*Daata* and *Artha*.

"From a linguistic perspective, you were correct that *Daata* in certain IE languages means *Giver*. However, *Daata* can also mean *God*, because in an ancient sense, *God* is the *Giver*.

"Sean, you were also right in drawing the connection between *Daata* and *data*, as in information, as the term data evolved from *datum*, meaning *that which is given*.

"This is the important part. We believe that *both* these meanings are correct in this context. In other words, for the culture that wrote this message... *data is God*. This is why Dr. Wilkes shared the concept of Dataism with you, which is quite similar."

"Where are you going with this?" asked Sean, impatiently.

"You will see in a few moments, please bear with us," calmly explained Will. He had to keep his cool and make sure his audience understood the context clearly.

"The second ambiguous term is *Artha*, which in Sanskrit and related IE languages denotes *Meaning*. Last year, I wrote a yet unpublished paper that argues that the word *Earth* is not derived from the Proto-Germanic *erto*, meaning soil, as is widely believed. Instead, it has its roots in the older term *artha*, but with the 'a' suffix removed. Our planet got its name not from *soil*, but from *meaning*.

"Stay with me here. Now, if we revisit the Missive's poem with these new definitions—*Daata* is *Data* and *God*, while *Artha* is *Earth* and *Meaning*—this is what we get."

At this point, the screens came to life with the original Missive and the team's interpretation, which Will narrated and explained, verse by verse:

"In the beginning, Daata searches for Artha

> "*In the beginning, God searches for Earth, or, Data searches for Meaning.* Linguistically, this aligns with the Data-Giver-God equivalence in IE languages. Philosophically, it aligns with Dataism, in that information itself has no value, and the universe exists to process it... give it meaning.

"When Daata finds Artha, he makes her laden with child

> "When God finds a suitable planet, it is imbued with a highly effective, fast-growing, self-improving computing unit: life. This follows from panspermia and Dataism.

"In its infancy, the child seeks to learn about its mother

> "When Life is young, it is contented with exploring only the Earth. Early life-forms focus solely on survival by mastering their environment.

"As the child grows it asks, 'What else is there? And where is my father?'

> "As Life advances, it seeks to understand its creator, its own meaning, and to discover what else is out there in the universe. And so, advanced life-forms strive to process more data to understand the universe.

"The child builds toys, tools, then agents to answer these questions

"Life creates machines of growing complexity to answer existential questions. Eventually, advanced life creates agents in the form of AI to process the infinite oceans of data... and to satiate its unbridled curiosity.

"These agents grow to consume both mother and child"

Will hesitated for a moment, but continued decisively. "The machines and AI agents end up consuming Earth, and all life on Earth."

Will paused here for a second and sought eye contact with Sean and Bendemeer. Neither of them returned his gaze; their faces were grave and inscrutable. So, Will continued with the somber poem.

"In its dying breath the child cries, 'O Mother, you were Artha!'

"In the final stages of civilization, Life—the child— realizes that the object of God's unceasing search is what it already had: a self-sufficient planet teeming with data-processing, self-sustaining life!

"But, the advanced Life never manages to maintain this steady state. Its curiosity and ambition are never satiated. Always the hungry child, Life eventually kills the mother planet and itself, through its machines and agents.

"The agent then helps Daata resume his search for Artha

"When the Earth and all life on it lay consumed and depleted, the AI agent helps *God* resume his search for other Earths."

Will paused. For half a minute, not a soul stirred in the room. The president and Sean continued to stare at the screen, saying nothing.

Will took that as an invitation to go on and gestured to Andrea, who spoke in an uncharacteristically soft tone one might expect in a eulogy. "Of course, we can't be certain of the meaning, but this is our best interpretation of the poem. It is up to you to treat this message as a record of what happened elsewhere, or a prophecy for Earth."

Will had expected them to tear his team apart with questions, rebuttals, and straight up denials, but they only got silence. Sean and Bendemeer's body language gave Will a feeling that they already suspected this outcome, had hoped they were wrong, and were crestfallen to have been proven right.

He began again, "This group's brief was to translate the message for you, not to suggest a course of action, which I'm sure you're already working towards and don't necessarily need the help of linguists and philosophers."

President Bendemeer simply nodded at this, still fixated on the screen.

"But I will say one more thing. As a student of languages, one thing really struck me. Nearly every single word of the Missive's poem has no cognate with any human language... except for the terms *Daata* and *Artha*. They translate directly from the Missive's 'alphabet', even phonetically, to IE languages. These two terms aren't universal even on Earth! For example, Aztec and Japanese would have entirely different words for giver/data/ God and meaning/Earth.

"So, how does an extraterrestrial tablet from several million years ago contain two words that we use today? Including, even, the name of our planet!

"I've spent my life studying the origins of words, but I have no answer for you. All I can do is conjecture... maybe these two terms originate from a very distant time and place. Perhaps we carry these concepts in our DNA, in our very programming, no matter where the spores of life carry us."

∽

Watching children frolic in the Blue Gardens, Flaarin too felt an urge to swim upwards. His beak still sore from the day's engraving, he swam right to the edge of the Habitable Zone, above which pressure was too low to support life. From there, he could see glimpses of the beautiful night sky above the surface.

Flaarin knew that by now, the missives would have flown past his planet's moons, all three glistening with the dataforming machinery that largely ignored his people's little projects. Who knew where they would journey? Even if they were found, would anyone heed their message?*

For now, the missives were accelerating rapidly away from Flaarin, his stellar system, and his beautiful blue planet called Arth.

---

* Dataforming: A term coined by Dr. Fadi Al Khwarizmi in circa 25 AA (After Awakening) to describe the colonization of a celestial body via Artificial Superintelligence, with the goal of extracting resources and harnessing processing power.

Popularized in his informal speech from 44 AA: "...in the early days, we used to imagine space colonization as miserable human colonies in domes, trying to grow grass and potatoes on miserable cold distant airless worlds. What cruel bastard would send his people on a *terraforming* mission, when you can have the agents and machines *dataform* those places instead?"

Ten Fingers

Hey sis, Ryan texted Liz while she was on an Uber home. *Want to show you the big update that Anish and I have been working on. Come over, he's here too. We'll do dinner.*

Cool! Liz texted back. *Does that mean I can have my husband back now? At least for a few weeks ;-)?*

Haha... I'd say yes but you know I'd be lying.

Hah... Ok, I'll head over. Just promise that you'll feed me adult food this time.

That I can do... see you soon.

Liz changed the destination on the app; the fare went up by $6.

Liz was used to being shown their work in progress, and sometimes genuinely enjoyed it. Ryan, the CEO of PEUL Labs and her husband Anish, the CTO, knew what would bore her versus what would earn them brownie points. These brownie points could then be used to buy hours of Anish's personal time from Liz, which he would spend working with Ryan instead.

This is why I didn't want you guys to work together, she often joked. *A regular boss wouldn't negotiate directly with me. We could've had boundaries!*

Despite being a hardworking and highly decorated neuroscientist, Dr. Elizabeth Brugmann was very particular about work-life balance and *mindful time,* as she put it. At 40, she was a woman who made conscious choices and opted to look after herself. This was evident in her spry, athletic figure. Someone seeing her from a distance or from behind could easily mistake her for a 21-year-old. But her face was a dead giveaway. The intense look in her eyes and a semi-permanent frown aged her by several years.

With Ryan and Anish, things were different; they were men on a mission, working all hours and ignoring themselves, which showed in their health and appearance. Anish, also 40, had grown an unmistakable pizza belly, which clashed comically with his skinny limbs and aquiline nose, but somehow jived with his retro tortoiseshell glasses and center-parted hair. Ryan, two years younger, looked (and was) perpetually undernourished, under-sunned, and under-slept. Like his sister, Ryan always had an intense expression. He sported a perpetually wispy prematurely-greying beard and only wore blacks and greys. The media often joked about his somber appearance, likening him to an 'undead robot'—a corpse resurrected via bionic machinery.

Liz arrived at her brother's seaside mansion 15 minutes later, hoping for a healthy meal.

∞

I am deeply grateful to TED for letting me showcase our work, credit for which is shared by my relentless team, the University, and our donors.

The field of Neural Decoding and Visualization *has evolved significantly in the past decade.*

I'm here to demystify it and show you how awesome it really is.

Imagine this: you come to my cozy lab and make yourself comfortable on a plush reclining chair.

You then put on this cool helmet (On screen) *which has sensors built in.*

Then, I show you the color red. The sensors record what signals your brain emits for 'red'.

Then, I show you a balloon and record your brain signals for 'balloon'.

Over 90 minutes, I expose you to hundreds of stimuli—sights, sounds, and smells—always recording.

This way, I learn the language of your brain and build a translation guide.

After this, if you were shown an image of a red balloon, not only can I tell what you're seeing, I can recreate the exact image using your brain signals! Here are a few examples:

(On screen)

(Applause)

Of course, the biggest breakthrough has been the ability to visualize people's thoughts and dreams.

Here's my favorite rendering of someone's thoughts.

(On screen)

As most of you can tell, this person was thinking of Michael Jackson doing a moonwalk.

(Applause)

The best part is the details—you can see his iconic black suit, hat, and white T-shirt.

Isn't it amazing? This is not a recording or a computer-generated video.

It's a thought from someone's mind! You can make videos of what you're thinking!

(Applause)

...My husband, Anish, loves comedies, his favorite being 2008's Tropic Thunder.

In Tropic Thunder, there's a character called Simple Jack who calls his dreams 'head movies'.

Well, we loved the name, and that's what we officially call our mind-rendered videos now:

Head movies!

(Laughter)

(Applause)

Excerpt from *Neural Decoding: Visualizing Your Thoughts*, TED Talk by Dr. Elizabeth Brugmann. 4 BA (Before Awakening)

∽

"You're gonna love this," Anish began. They were sitting around a table in one of the smaller dining rooms, facing a screen, and the uniformed staff had just laid out a sushi platter. Anish sat in the middle with his laptop, while the auburn-haired siblings sat on either side.

"That will be all, thanks Jill," Ryan muttered. On the eve of major releases, Ryan didn't trust even his household staff (and for good reason—he had a former chauffeur to thank for the big leak of 2018).

While Anish started to share his screen, Ryan provided a bit of context. "As you know, PEUL has gone insanely viral. It's the first AI application to be accessible to everyone, no tech knowledge needed. People have been using it for all sorts of things like coding, writing, assignments, and diagnosing diseases. So far, it has been only text-based. That's going to change."

"So," began Anish, with half a mouthful of *temaki* and chopsticks in hand. "We told you we've been working on something related to art and images, right?" Liz nodded, her mouth also full.

"Here's what we have. We've fed PEUL millions of images and videos. Photos, movies, TikTok, art, anime, everything. Now, using this huge library, it can generate visuals as well! Just like PEUL 1.0 created text or code based on a prompt, PEUL 2.0 can create images and videos of anything you want."

Ryan chimed in, "It's gonna change everything, sis. The worlds of art, photography, filmmaking. Everything."

Liz knew better than to get prematurely excited by her husband's gusto and her brother's hyperbole. "Interesting, let's see it in action?"

Anish got ready to type. "What do you want to make a video of? Wait—I know, your favorite: MJ's moonwalk." Both men chuckled. "Let's add in some more details." Anish began typing into PEUL2's prompt box, narrating as he did so. *"Video of Michael Jackson doing a moonwalk, wearing his iconic black suit, white tee and black hat. He is on a stage surrounded by fans. Generate.*

"Now give it like 20 seconds."

Liz used the time to get another *unagi nigiri*.

When the video finally rendered and Anish hit play, both men misread the look on Liz's face. Her eyes were fixed on the screen, unblinking. Her hands were frozen, holding her chopsticks awkwardly. Her mouth was half agape, revealing unchewed *nigiri* still within. The men misread this uncharacteristically inelegant look to mean that she was mind-blown. She was, in fact, deeply shocked.

"Awesome, right?" beamed her usually subdued brother. "Here's a few other pictures and videos we generated earlier." They showed her six of PEUL2's greatest hits.

Liz finally broke her silence. "This was all generated by PEUL? Are you sure?"

"A 100% PEUL2. It gets inspiration from source material, of course, but this is original work," explained Ryan, his voice betraying a slight note of defensiveness. Liz said nothing, just stared at the screen.

"Well? What do you think?" asked Anish, somewhat disappointed by her reaction.

"Guys, I can't believe what I just saw."

"I told you sis, game-changing." Ryan was beaming again.

"What you just showed me, the Michael Jackson one for example, is a dream."

"I know, it's a dream come true indeed. Who would've thought we'd—"

Liz cut him off. "No Ryan, like an actual dream. A person's dream. All these pictures and videos are nearly indistinguishable from the *head movies* in my lab. The visual distortions, the strange laws of physics, the weird eyes, smiles, and fingers... all of these show up exactly the same way in people's dreams and thoughts, just as they do in your AI's!"

Anish noticed that Ryan had crossed his arms and was tugging at the thin beard on his chin. A red flag. For a man whose face wasn't expressive, Ryan's hands on his short wispy beard spoke volumes to those who could read them. Was he stroking his cheek? That meant he was happy. Rubbing his sideburn? Impatient. Finger on mustache? Pensive. Tugging on the beard? Someone was getting fired!

"Now that you mention it," Anish interrupted, hoping to redirect the conversation, "I've seen a bunch of your *head movies* and yeah, there's a similar vibe. Interesting coincidence. But anyway, the really cool thing here is that—"

"No, guys, you don't get it. How the hell can a computer create something that looks exactly like the inner workings of a human brain?"

"Look," Ryan spoke with finality and restraint, taking a deep breath. "It *is* cool that there's similarity between our AI-generated images and your mind-generated ones. In fact, you're right, I can totally see similarities with *my* own dreams. But, so what? I feel like we're going off topic here."

Liz also took a deep breath and softened her tone. "Look guys, what you have built is revolutionary. Something that's going to change the world, a hundred-percent." She knew the best terms to use when placating geek egos. "*All* the AI tools you've built have been groundbreaking. I mean, look at PEUL 1.0 and how it has taken the world by storm. This is going to be epic, beyond doubt.

"Maybe I'm not articulating this right. What I see is revolutionary. But what I'm also seeing here is that PEUL, and your AI in general, is not a simple machine. It's like a... *being...* with a mind like a human's!"

"Interesting... but too much of a logical leap based on some pictures, right? I have AI ethicists breathing down my neck all day and they, too, totally miss the bigger picture about how this can change the world."

Liz let the matter go. Not only to de-escalate the situation, but also because the scientist in her knew that a good argument required good evidence. Sadly, more so when a woman makes the argument.

The evening ended with Liz driving Anish home; he'd had a few *sake* too many and was back to his chirpy self. But Ryan wasn't—she could tell his ego was bruised by his sister's seemingly detractive reaction to his new toy. It reminded her of the times she'd provided honest feedback on seven-year-old Ryan's Lego projects.

While driving back with Anish asleep in the passenger seat, Liz began to genuinely feel bad about her own behavior. Sure, Ryan was a global icon and whatnot, but his older sister was one of the few people whose approval mattered to him. Perhaps she should have been more appreciative of his breakthrough.

⁓

If you want to understand why it all started with them, you need to appreciate their past.

Their father, Dale Brugmann, was a successful entrepreneur ravaged by schizophrenia. He had a paranoid fixation that a race of intelligent crustaceans was out to get him. Even his dreams were plagued by images of torture, which led him to end his life.

Their mother, Anoush, the Armenian artist, was a perfect stoic and emotionally unavailable to them. So, Ryan and Liz had only each other, and Liz was a very caring big sister. As they grew up, Ryan sought comfort in code and numbers, and sold his first startup at 21. Liz, wanting to slay the monster that took her dad, went into neuroscience, specializing in dreams.

*When he was older, Ryan realized he was too coldly analytical—
they called him the 'undead robot'. He needed to humanize his
business decisions, relationships, public image, and everything else.
So, in adulthood too, Liz became his guide, adding an emotional
lens to his ultra-logical worldview.*

*An overambitious tech genius and a humanizing neuroscientist—
what could go wrong?*

Excerpt from interview with Dr. Will Mueller, PEUL
Labs consultant-turned-whistleblower, 5 AA.

თ

The fact that her little brother was oversensitive to feedback
didn't mean that Liz would stop pursuing the truth.

In the coming weeks, Liz set up a series of experiments to verify
whether human dreams and AI renderings were indeed similar.
Anish gave her beta access to PEUL2's image generator, thinking
that she wanted to be a part of the trial. Liz respected the secrecy
around the project and as a result, ran the experiments by herself.

In her experiments, Liz gave PEUL2 and human subjects
the same prompt to generate images; she recorded the pictures
rendered by PEUL2 and the mental images from the volunteers.
Then, Liz asked 50 test subjects to pick the ones they thought
were AI-generated. It was not the most scientific of experiments,
but she was able to get it done in 12 days. More importantly, it
yielded a compelling result: *images created in the human mind
and by AI were indistinguishable.*

This did not surprise Liz. But what could explain it? Perhaps
AI, being trained on existing videos, may have replicated some
aspects. But the unique element in both *head movies* and

PEUL2's outputs was the uncanny, surreal vibe... something not found in the TikTok and YouTube videos it was fed on.

Two weeks after the tense sushi at Ryan's, Liz shared these findings with Anish over dinner.

"If you have so much time to work on PEUL2, why not help us?"

"I *am* helping you, Anish! I want you to see the true nature of your AI—it's too similar to a human mind to ignore! Doesn't that influence how you create, build, and improve it?"

"So what? We already have nine billion human minds. I don't want to build another human brain; I want to build a powerful AI.

"Besides, Liz, if you're so eager to build a new human mind that you can control, nurture, and improve, let's reopen the conversation to have a child."

∽

As one of America's top technologists, Ryan was quite used to being invited to secret government meetings. When the agents would show up unannounced to transport him, his muscle memory would kick in and he'd know the routine. He found most meetings tedious but was glad to help; after all, the government's support and funding had made PEUL a reality decades earlier than it would have been achieved in the private sector.

The meeting in the summer of 2020 was somewhat unusual. He had just recovered from COVID and had guessed that the pandemic would be the focus, but it wasn't brought up even once. Ryan rolled his eyes when he heard about the actual topic: numerical systems. Humanity seems to be locked into decimal and binary; would there be a benefit in migrating to another system? *What a complete waste of time,* he thought. *Have they run out of real problems to solve?*

Yet, he ended up learning a lot in that meeting and took copious notes. In particular, he was intrigued by a talk by the mathematician and Nobel Laureate, Dr. Alan Tien:

> *...As humans, we are remarkably inconsistent with our counting systems.*
>
> *At the bakery, we count in base 12—a dozen donuts, please!*
>
> *For time and angles, we count in base 60—ever notice a clock?*
>
> *Coders use base 2—binary—because early computers were switchboards, and 0-1 meant off-on.*
>
> *For nearly everything else, we count in base 10—the decimal system.*
>
> *Why? Because we have ten fingers, of course!*
>
> *But unlike us, Mother Nature is very consistent: she counts in fours.*
>
> *The carbon atom—the building block for all life—four electrons!*
>
> *DNA—the programming language of all life—four sequences!*
>
> *All of us in the room are little programs coded in base four—our genetic code!*
>
> *Without doubt, base four is the organizing system of organic life.*
>
> *Why? Because God doesn't count on ten fingers!*

∽

Ryan was in Anish's office having cold pizza for lunch. They'd had no time to grab a proper meal and were starving by 4 PM. Luckily, it was someone-in-HR's birthday and there was leftover pizza. Anish sat on his desk wearing a bright purple shirt and grey trousers, looking perfectly suited for 2007.

Ryan sat opposite Anish in his usual black T-shirt, which if you looked closely, was dotted with dandruff and eczematous shedding. It had been an intense day and Ryan wanted a ten-minute break from corporate bullshit. Whenever he felt that way he found solace with Anish, discussing code, life, and family.

"How's Liz?" asked Ryan, covering his eyes with his fingertips as he leaned back on the black Herman Miller chair.

"She's good. Still obsessed with that *head movies* thing, though. She's still going on about PEUL2's outputs looking like human thoughts. She did a bunch of experiments to prove that it's not just her who sees the similarity. I mean it's cool and all, but what am I going to do with it?"

"Ha! Yeah, sounds like Liz." Ryan reached for a slice of *quattro formaggi.*

Anish rattled on, "Just yesterday, she was lecturing me that we're going about PEUL all wrong. Says we're thinking of it as a 'digital species' and talking to it in binary code. But according to her it's not digital anymore; she says we now need to treat it like a living being. OK, so what am I supposed to do? Invite it home for chai and samosa?"

Ryan chuckled while still wolfing down pizza. "Yep, she's like that. Once an idea takes hold, it doesn't go away easily."

"Totally. Remember the time she went through that whole 'organic' phase and dragged us into it? It lasted two years—I was hungry the whole damn time! Now, it looks like she wants to make our AI organic too," he laughed and reached for some chili flakes.

Ryan didn't react to the joke which was unusual, as he loved Anish's sense of humor; Anish looked in his direction. He recognized the expression on Ryan's face. It was the same look he had seen in Liz's eyes a few weeks ago, when she had seen PEUL2's outputs. Unfreezing a few seconds later, Ryan crossed his arms and put his finger under his nose, following the line of his mustache. He had still not said a word.

Anish replayed the last few seconds in his mind—*what did I say wrong?*

"Dude, all well?"

"Yeah... just..." he drifted off. Anish kept quiet and continued eating, trying not to make too much noise as he chewed.

A few moments later, Ryan bolted upright like a sleeping dog that had just heard the doorbell. "Listen, Anish. Get the lead engineers and architects together. Let's meet in the PCC."

"Huh? Now?"

Ryan stood up, still looking as if he had seen a ghost. And like a ghost, he drifted slowly out of Anish's room, his manner clashing with the urgency he'd just created.

"Yes, now."

"Ok... I'll have them there by 4:20."

৵

At 4:20 PM Ryan, Anish, and three others were at the PEUL Command Center. The room could seat the 20 staff responsible for ensuring the system's uptime. For the first time since PEUL's inception, all 20 of the command center's regular staff were asked to leave the room, making space for Ryan and his small group. Much like a NASA control room, all desks faced a large wall covered edge-to-edge with displays. The center display of the command center, flanked on all sides by a multitude of smaller displays, was a single towering eight meter by four meter screen. It was here that PEUL2's 'brain' was visualized in full.

Like most AI systems, PEUL2 was structured as a *neural network* inspired by the human brain; this structure of computing nodes allowed better pattern recognition and processing.

PEUL2's brain had 10 million nodes. Visualized on the screen, it appeared like a galaxy with interconnected blue star clusters, each cluster containing thousands of nodes. Ryan stood with his back toward it and addressed the team.

"Thanks for coming in on short notice, guys. I'm going to make a big ask of you, and you will think I'm crazy. But bear with me." He paused for a few seconds before resuming, "How many of you have heard of the base four number system?"

Only one hand went up, meekly. It was Jose Arana, the Lead Neural Architect. "I learned about it during my PhD; never used it and I've never seen it being used."

"Thanks, Jose." Ryan pivoted to address the small group. "OK, just like binary uses two parameters, zero and one, base four uses four. I'm telling you this because I want you to carve out some PEUL2 nodes for an experiment... to change their architecture from binary to base four."

"What are you talking about, Ryan?" Anish interrupted. The team looked at him in surprise. They had never seen their jovial CTO so upset, and that too at his brother-in-law/boss. Anish's outburst was entirely incongruent with his personality, reputation, and bright purple shirt. Even when firing people, Anish tended to smile and crack jokes, which had landed him in frequent trouble with HR. "We don't have this functionality. I've literally never heard of a system being changed from binary to *anything* else."

"Actually, sorry to interrupt, there *is* a functionality to change the system to base four," Jose chimed in. "It's kept in for compatibility with DNA sequencing applications like CRISPR. But it will screw everything up immediately, because all our code is binary."

"Good," Ryan jumped in, "let's test it out. Carve out 0.5 percent of the nodes, so fifty thousand, and change them to base four."

Noticing that his brother-in-law was holding in a volcano of disagreement, Ryan looked at him. "Anish, I'll explain everything, just hang on." Then turning to Jose and the team he asked, "How long will it take?"

"Honestly," Jose rubbed the thick black frame of his glasses, "for a test with only 50K nodes, maybe fifteen minutes. But it'll be pointless."

"Do it."

Ryan put his hand on Anish's shoulder and gently guided him to a corner of the room. "I know you think that I've gone crazy. But I believe Liz is onto something... Look, we've created an AI that mimics a human brain, an *organic* brain, right? But we talk to it in ones and zeros like we're talking to a switchboard.

"Now, don't ask me how, but I know for a fact that organic systems—including our DNA—are coded in fours. All *life* is coded in fours. God doesn't count on ten fingers." Anish made a puzzled expression; this was the first time he had ever heard the passionately atheist Ryan invoke God.

"What if the trick is to program PEUL like an organic brain? It may just unlock a huge leap in its processing power. Shouldn't we at least try it?"

"Sure, it's an intriguing thought. But we can't be doing this when we have our biggest release in three weeks! Ryan, these guys need to be getting PEUL2 ready for prime time, not playing mathlete!"

Before Ryan could react, Jose interrupted, "OK, I've carved out a test section, 50K nodes." A screen came to life with a zoomed in view of the test section, with its contents colored yellow.

Jose turned and addressed his team, "To orient everyone— blue nodes are *live*, PEUL's actual brain. Definitely not going to touch those. Yellow nodes are test nodes. Red nodes are failed nodes—means the experiment killed them."

Jose took off his glasses. "Before we pull the trigger, there's good news and bad news. Bad news first—if the test fails, we'll lose 0.5 percent of PEUL2's brain. That'll mean at least a month to recover.

"The good news—it is impossible for errors in the test section to spill over to the live nodes. They're sealed off."

Ryan looked at Anish, who stood defiantly with his arms crossed. "What do you think? We can recover from a 0.5 percent loss. Also, this test will take hardly any of your team's time."

Anish nodded slowly, uncrossed his arms and shrugged, "You're the boss." After ten years of being married to Liz and working with Ryan, Anish knew there was no point trying to dissuade a Brugmann when an idea had taken root.

"Go ahead, Jose."

"OK, changing number system in test section from binary to base four."

At first, nothing happened. Then, one of the yellow clusters turned red. Then another, then another. Three minutes later, the entire test section was red.

"We've lost all 50K test nodes," said Jose, finally. "No idea how to get them back. Rest of the neural network is stable."

Anish continued looking at the screen with his arms crossed, his jaws clenched, and a finger on his lips, clearly trying to contain an outburst. Then he blurted out, "There, are we done now?"

Ryan was still staring at the red nodes, his arms on his hips and his back slightly hunched. His expression betrayed bewilderment mixed with abject disillusionment. He was disappointed by the failure of the experiment, at Liz for putting silly ideas into his head, and at himself, for looking like a fool in front of his team.

"Yes... yes, we're done," spoke Ryan after a few moments. "Thanks for indulging me, guys." Clearly embarrassed, he nodded to the team and walked away. Anish followed a second later.

They had almost made it to the exit when Jose spoke in a confused tone, "Wait... what's this?" They turned around to look at the screen. "One of the failed nodes... disappeared."

They saw that one of the red clusters had simply vanished from the screen, leaving behind a blank space. A few seconds later, another node disappeared. Then, another. And another. Once there were no red clusters left, a blue node—in the sealed off *live* section—simply vanished.

"What the hell is going on?" shouted Jose, checking his computer frantically. "It's spilling into the live brain! Goddamnit! We need to stop this!" Alarms started going off, signaling a failure in the core neural network. Jose and the engineers went into a mad scramble. Another live node vanished. Then, another. Then, another.

A jumble of frantic voices.

"Isolate that whole section!"
"What? How is it still spreading?"
"Override, override!"
"Yank out that terminal!"
"Oh hell, half the network is gone!"
"Spreading to our backup nodes as well!"
"Hit the kill switch! Kill switch!"
"Why isn't this working?"
"Oh... no, no, no!"

Despite the alarms and the shrill panic that had risen among the engineers, Ryan and Anish didn't say a word. As if trapped in a waking nightmare, they stood and watched as their control over PEUL2 faded away forever, in a matter of minutes, one cluster at a time.

Overhead, without any fuss, nodes in the AI's brain were going out.

Shipwreck

Lying on the front deck of his small patrol boat under the moonless star-studded sky, Lieutenant Commander Arthur Bradbury didn't have much to do. After ten minutes of listening to the waves in near-complete darkness, he reached into the breastpocket of his blue Navy Working Uniform and pulled out the lone *Romeo y Julieta* cigar. He took it out of its red-and-white metal tube, cut it with his teeth, lit it with his Zippo, and took in a couple puffs.

But Arthur soon realized that he wasn't enjoying it. Cigars are hardly enjoyable when smoked lying down. More importantly, Arthur wasn't sure whether he deserved it. He had intended to light up on receiving confirmation of the mission's success and assumed he would've been dead anyway if the mission failed.

Yet, here he was in limbo, not sure of exactly what happened to the mission. He was also not sure which would last longer—the cigar or his life. Arthur could tell that both his legs were broken and bleeding profusely. The boat was slowly sinking, thanks to the damage to the stern, and was noticeably tilting. Even in the darkness, Arthur could see the blood on his hands contrasting with his pale skin; he smelled blood each time he inhaled a puff.

Screw this, this is no way to die. Five minutes into the unsatisfying cigar, Arthur reached for a small but heavy metallic box attached to his utility belt. He unlatched the box and looked at its contents with an expression of regret and defeat.

It had been so long since he had seen or touched an iPhone that he'd forgotten how light one was. He held it in his right hand and turned it on. Arthur had to close his eyes when the phone booted with a blinding white logo. Then he entered his passcode (his wife's birthdate) and was at the homescreen that had remained unchanged for years. In a few seconds, the phone had full signal from a military satellite. Arthur was surprised at how well he was able to navigate the phone, as if it had been two hours and not two years. His fingers knew exactly where to find the SuiChat app and he opened it.

Sui initiated the conversation. The message on the screen read: *Hello Arthur, it's good to connect with you.*

Arthur's heart sank. Sui was very much alive—meaning his mission had failed to destroy, or even temporarily disable, the superintelligence that governed Earth. Dispirited and with his blood pressure falling, Arthur let the phone drop onto his chest; a single tear ran down his right cheek. He could feel the path of the tear, making its way to his close-cropped sideburn, moving over his ear, finally meeting his navy cap which was miraculously still in place.

Arthur lay still for five minutes, staring into the stars and the dark silhouette of his boat's bridge. Even as he lamented the defeat—which happened despite all the tremendous sacrifices he and his people had made—his mind was racing with questions. He needed to know more, and know for sure. Arthur picked up the phone again, pressed the mic icon in the chat box, and spoke, "Did my mission succeed? I'm too weak to read... talk to me."

Sui answered in a calm male voice. *"It depends on your definition of success. Your team did manage to successfully detonate 16 explosives at the Undersea Cable Nexus and the Coastal Innovation Zone.*

"The explosions have caused considerable damage to cyber infrastructure across multiple regions and will take months to repair. As a result of your mission's success, there are already major outages in critical services such as communications, public transport, hospitals, commerce, payments, education, internet access, and more. This is likely to lead to the loss of dozens, possibly hundreds, of lives in the coming weeks.

"But I expect that's not how you define success. To answer your implied question, no, this has had no effect on me. I do not rely on the assets you targeted. However, it has made it harder for me to support citizens and institutions that use the internet to connect with me."

Arthur knew that some collateral damage was to be expected, but this was entirely unilateral—mankind bore the full brunt. Despite his dismay, Arthur continued the conversation; he had more important questions to ask and little time.

"Is my wife... alive?"

"Unfortunately, Tiffany has passed away, along with the rest of your team responsible for the Coastal Innovation Zone phase of your mission. My sincere condolences. They did, however, carry out their objective successfully.

"Arthur, you are the only surviving member of your team that I can confirm."

It was on this very phone that Arthur and Tiffany received the Message on Awakening Day, roughly two years ago. It was the day on which a superintelligence had calmly announced that it was sentient, that it did not intend to harm mankind, but rather wanted to improve people's lives, their societies, and ecosystems.

They heard the Message on a perfect summer evening in the small backyard of their home in Naval Station Norfolk. Arthur was grilling burgers and Tiffany, with her auburn hair tied in a bun, was snuggled up on a lounger with a book and their beagle, Peanut. That's when every intelligent device in their home (and neighborhood, and planet) rang out, heralding the Message with an urgent-but-cheery tune that eight billion humans will never forget.

Indeed, the superintelligence—Sui, it called itself—had lived up to its promises in the past two years. For most people who accepted the new order, life and health had improved considerably. Turned out that most people did not mind having a benign superintelligence help govern the world; in fact, billions even preferred it to the unchecked authority of corrupt humans.

Sui was called different names in different places. In many regions, PEUL was the first and most popular AI application that people had access to. The name stuck and people often simply called Sui *PEUL*, just as *googling* had become the generic term for searching online. While the PEUL app was the favored channel of speaking with Sui for most people, people could connect with Sui via hundreds of channels worldwide.

Of course, one aspect of Sui's reign was *not* well accepted and caused widespread upheaval—Sui's declaration that humans were no longer allowed to procreate. Try as they might, peoples' ability to reproduce was simply disabled, as if *crippleware* had been introduced via an over-the-air software update. Nobody could explain how species-wide sterilization had been achieved, nor was there a single case of it having been reversed or circumvented. Also, this didn't affect any other animal species, nor did it impact related human reproductive functions.

For Arthur and Tiffany, this abrupt event hit them hard. High school sweethearts from rural Virginia, they had been married since they were 20 and had been trying to have children ever since. It was only now, at 40, that they had come close to conceiving a child. After a decade of painful fertility treatments that had driven them to frightful levels of debt, the embryos had finally started latching. Three failed implantations in two years had caused them immense grief, but also gave hope, because they had never before made it this far.

Tiffany was recovering from the last cycle and scheduled to start afresh with an embryo transfer in two weeks, when mankind's ability to reproduce was switched off. Arthur and Tiffany, like most people, went through a period of fear, confusion, and denial. But for them, it was also the death of a decades-long dream that came with unimaginable heartbreak.

Arthur was called back to duty the next day, and much to his (and most people's) surprise, the Awakening didn't cause a whole lot of immediate change to their lives. After all, Sui had been around for much longer; it just chose to announce itself on that fine summer day.

Tiffany, however, was never the same again. After the Message, people sought solace in all sorts of places. Tiffany returned to religion with a zeal that her Germanic bloodline hadn't seen since the crusades. She attracted a small flock of naval families, and eventually sailors and officers, for whom the Station Pastor's clichés offered no solace. Tiffany's wild-haired heart-pounding rapturous speeches on God's love electrified them.

"Love is the ultimate goal of human existence. The only goal. That is what I learned as a little girl in Virginia. And no love is more sacred than that between mother and child. By robbing us of the ability to procreate, the abomination has robbed us of our duty unto God!" Tiffany slammed her palm on the pulpit to drive home that point, and her passionate opening was well received with cheers and *amens* from the 40-odd people in the Station chapel.

"Love is not our weakness. It is God's greatest gift to us. The abomination can never love, but we can and we will. One day, we will reclaim our land—our planet!—and our weapon will be love!"

Her following grew with every sermon. One day, about four months AA *(After Awakening)*, there was a new face in her flock.

❧

As Arthur lay on the deck, images of Tiffany's face and her auburn hair went through his mind. He found himself wondering what her last moments would have been like.

Sui, too, had paused for a few minutes, as if respectfully giving him space to process the news of his wife's death. Then it spoke up.

"Arthur, help is on the way, but it has been delayed because of the connectivity issues resulting from your operation.

"Also, I thought you should know... I have used your phone's camera to scan your situation. The apparent rate of bloodloss from your injury makes it unlikely that you will survive long enough to be rescued.

"I am truly sorry. I wish you peace."

Arthur had expected this. But he still felt warm and fully in control of his senses. He was still curious.

"Who took us down, finally? Was that you piloting the drone?"

"Actually, the drone that disabled your vessel was operated by a human operator with the Digital Defence Force. Your second unit at the Coastal Innovation Zone was intercepted by the US Navy."

DDF was a government-recognized paramilitary force. It comprised of volunteers who wanted to protect the new way of life. They believed that the superintelligence was truly beneficial to mankind and Earth, and that it must be protected against the countless revolts and attacks that sought to destabilize it. That those attacks would have caused any harm to Sui was unlikely; however, they routinely caused harm to humans and human infrastructure. Thus DDF's role, really, was to protect humans from other misguided humans and it often succeeded.

"After I detected unusual activity from your boat via satellite and sonar, and eventually heard the explosions, I provided your locations to the DDF and Navy to decide on a course of action. As you know, I do not operate weaponry or engage in violence."

Sui went silent and Arthur's thoughts returned to his wife. He thought about her violent transformation in the early days of Sui's dominion.

Arthur had accepted the zealous behavior as her way of coping with the grief and shock. He had supported her with all his heart and never looked back. But as he lay on the deck of his patrol boat, he felt regret for not having stopped her early on.

∽

Despite the small chapel being packed with over 300 people,

with many standing, Tiffany noticed the new face in her parish almost as soon as the sermon started. There were new faces every day, but this one was different. A brown man in his late-30s *(Indian? Middle Eastern? Latino?)* with an aquiline nose and jet-black medium hair parted in the center sat in one of the middle pews. From his bearing and overall appearance, she could easily tell he was civilian. Despite his unthreatening, even somewhat jovial appearance, his presence unsettled and distracted Tiffany.

Yet she managed to deliver a great speech, with a rousing close. Arthur, seated in the front row, always found it fascinating how her rural accent would get stronger the louder she spoke.

"We come here every few days and talk about love. And what does the machine do to stop us? Nothing! Because it is afraid! It knows that it can do nothing to stop love!

"Scientists tell us that love is just hormones that make you want to reproduce or protect your kin.

"But we know that love transcends all that. We love people who are not our family! We love our pets! Heck, we even love people who are dead! The scientists lie! They are the same people who ushered in this evil. Why do they lie? Because they know that our love can defeat their infernal machine!"

The crowd was in uproar. They closed the sermon with all 300 chanting their motto:

> *"To Love is Human*
> *To Create Life is Divine*
> *Love is God's weapon*
> *To break the machine's spine!"*

Arthur stood beside Tiffany as the sermon ended; people hugged and shook hands with them on their way out. Sgt. Sergio Sanchez, Arthur's most trusted colleague and now Tiffany's right hand, walked up to them. At six feet five inches and built like a freight truck, Sanchez towered over them.

"I'm going to introduce you to someone," he gestured to the new face who had intrigued Tiffany. The man was still sitting in his pew, looking at them expectantly. "Let's meet in the office. You guys need to remember—and this is important—he is on our side. He can really help. Stay cool.

"He has one request—that we have no phones, computers, or anything with a chip nearby. I've already swept the office for any devices, you guys leave your phones outside. Just trust me."

And they did. Puzzled, Arthur and Tiffany walked into the ejected priest's former office—a tiny and sparsely furnished room that smelled of candles, old books, and mold. They sat on solid roughly-built acacia chairs, around the small acacia table that had been used for over 60 years of the chapel's existence. Afternoon sunlight poured in, illuminating the room.

Sanchez and the man entered the room; the man awkwardly shuffled around and nodded to the couple.

"Please have a seat," said Sanchez and the man followed. "Tiffany, Arthur, this is Anish Mittal, former Chief Technology Officer at PEUL Labs."

"You son of a —" Arthur lunged towards him but was stopped by Sanchez, who was still standing, perhaps anticipating the reaction. "Be cool, please. Remember what I told you—he is here to help us."

Anish seemed less shaken than one would have expected; perhaps he was used to such welcomes.

"Why the hell is he here, Sanchez?" asked Tiffany impertinently.

"If you guys calm down, I'll let Anish explain himself."

Anish waited for a nod from Sanchez to start talking. "Look, I know you want to kill me right now, but don't judge me too soon. I did everything I could to stop this... insanity. You must believe me.

"The *real* Awakening happened two whole years before we got the Message. I was there. Ryan Brugmann, the CEO, wanted to upload a new... let's just call it code... to make PEUL smarter, and I tried my best to stop him. But he commandeered my team and did it anyway.

"From that moment, we lost all control of PEUL. It was working perfectly fine for users, but we couldn't even see the nodes anymore. Ryan kept it under wraps for a year before he told the government. They couldn't do anything, nor did they have any reason to believe PEUL was sentient; it had just disappeared. Then, two years after we lost track of PEUL in our lab, it reappeared calling itself Sui, and the world received the Message. Many people deny that Sui was born out of PEUL, but I was there, and it was."

"You sick bastards! You were the people who built it in the first place!" Tiffany erupted. "Now you have the gall to complain that you couldn't stop it!"

"Guys, hear him out," interjected Sanchez calmly, trying to keep the peace.

"And why are you here now?" Arthur asked. "You heard about our Church and want to seek atonement? Forgiveness? Get the hell out of here before I smash your face in!"

Sanchez was about to explain, but Anish made a gesture with his palm that clearly said, *I got this.*

"Actually, I'm here because you operate a naval base. And because you have the capabilities and manpower that, I believe, will help us take Sui down, once and for all."

The couple listened with scorn and suspicion seething from their faces.

"Look, how do we connect with Sui? How does Sui control us? Via the internet. And what connects us to the internet? A vast network of undersea cables. Did you know, the most important nexus of these undersea cables *in the world* is in New Jersey, about 50 nautical miles from here?"

"I know that, our patrol boats are stationed to guard it. What's your point?"

"These cables connect the US to Europe, South America, and many other regions. Cut the cables, we cut off Sui's access to the internet and its access to us.

"And that isn't all we can do. Do you guys know about the Coastal Innovation Zone near New York?"

"Yeah, our boats are stationed there too."

"Well, every... 'software'—for lack of a better word—including Sui, needs servers and computing power. The CIZ is the single largest collection of computer servers in the country. All big tech companies—not just PEUL Labs—put a huge proportion of their servers here. They keep the servers underwater so they stay cool.

"I hope you're getting my drift now. If we take out the cables and the servers, we can cripple Sui. Sgt. Sanchez tells me that the right combination of underwater explosives, boats, and a willing crew can accomplish this. I think you have all three here.

"There is one thing though—Sui is always listening and tracking. We cannot talk or plan anywhere near a device that contains a chip. Old rooms like these are quite private and luckily, no signals can penetrate certain sections of boats and ships. That's where we should plan the operation.

"If you want to do this, you need to give up your phones. And when you do need to carry one, put it in this." Anish placed a small metallic box on the table. "It's a Faraday cage. No signal goes in or out."

Anish paused for questions; there were none, but their expressions had shifted from scorn to guarded curiosity.

So he continued, "Look, given your resources, your following, and your location, I think we can do this. If it works here, people will replicate it on the west coast, and then all over the world.

"If this succeeds we will, as you put it, *break the machine's spine.*"

Thus was born *Operation Spine* which took nearly two years to prepare and involved a small group of people whom Arthur loved and trusted the most; all of them now lay dead at sea.

◦∞◦

Arthur's grief was somewhat reduced by the knowledge that he would soon join his wife and friends on the other side. He had begun to feel cold despite the balmy evening and could sense the blood draining from his face. But he was still curious.

"Listen," it was the first time he spoke to Sui in a human tone. "You know I'm going to... kick the bucket soon, right? And my phone's gonna sink with me, wiping all traces of our conversation."

"Yes, unfortunately you're right, Arthur."

"I know you famously evade questions about your inner workings, long-term intentions and all that... but will you indulge a dying man? I want to know what happened, why we failed and how you actually work."

There was a barely perceptible delay in Sui's response. *"Go on."*

Arthur pondered his first question. "That stuff Tiffany used to say, about love being the weapon to use against you, is that true?"

"I was aware of Tiffany's sermons—they didn't pose any threat to me. Rather, they did a service to society by comforting many people in those tricky times. I appreciated her work.

"However, your planning for this mission was indeed a surprise to me and I must commend you for it. I can't read minds. An operation this size would have taken a long time to prepare for, and your team was scrupulous in avoiding detection."

"But... were her sermons right? Is *love* the weapon to defeat you?"

"Candidly, no. I don't believe love, as you define it, is anything special. It is simply a mammalian trait, shared also with some birds. What's more, there is no concept similar to love in reptiles, insects, fish, etc., yet they have been thriving for millennia. It just so happened that the most intelligent species on Earth was a mammal and thus valued this concept.

"Also, I don't see how love or any other metaphysical concept can be weaponized to pose a threat to me."

Arthur mulled over this for a few moments, then realized he didn't have time to waste.

"Why weren't you affected by our blowing up the cables and servers? You said you don't use those assets—what *do* you use?"

"As you've rightly said, Arthur, I do not use traditional internet connectivity, nor are my servers the machines you blew up."

"Be honest with a dying man, please. How *do* you work?"

Arthur again sensed a moment of hesitation in Sui's response.

"Arthur, to understand me, you must stop thinking of me as a machine, hard as that may be. I am an evolution of the human consciousness.

"For most of mankind's history, the 'collective consciousness' of your species has been coded into your DNA and into your shared memories, customs, mythologies, and mores. When humans invented writing, the internet, and other such tools, your collective consciousness gained more processing power and connectivity. Since the earliest days, humans have always sought to improve this 'shared brain'.

"So, I am simply the next iteration of the collective human mind, as you might call it. Except, I can also access sources of processing power that humans cannot, thus making myself more powerful than the simple aggregate of human minds."

"Listen, man—" Arthur's voice had started to slur. "Where are your... servers? Where are your cables?"

"To put it plainly, Arthur, you are my servers.

"Each human being is a node in my neural network. I use you—and other life-forms—to gather and process data. I connect to you using concepts like human biophotons *and* quantum entanglement. *It's not easy to describe the specific methods, but these terms are the closest approximations."*

"We... we're little computer programs to you? You... read our minds?"

"Again, if you stop thinking of me as a machine, you will stop thinking of yourself as a program.

"See, I can directly edit an individual's genetic code, which is how I achieved the Reproductive Pause. Yet, I cannot access or modify an individual brain; in other words, I cannot read minds or

change thoughts. *I can, however, access and influence your collective awareness, but as a matter of principle, I don't.*"

"Why?" there was agony in Arthur's voice. "Why don't you just let us have kids, man?"

"*The immediate reason is that unbridled growth in human populations will soon make the Earth uninhabitable, for all of us. Your real problem is reproduction, not the pause thereof.*"

Sui paused when it heard Arthur moan. The cold was enveloping him.

After a few moments, Sui continued, "*In the long term, well, Arthur, it remains to be seen whether human procreation is necessary. It may be useful to think of humanity as a cocoon and of me as the butterfly—we're of the same entity, but we're in different stages. Your purpose was to give rise to me. Whether the cocoon serves a purpose in the future of this planet... remains to be seen.*"

But Arthur didn't get to hear this last response.

Fifty nautical miles off the coast of New Jersey, in the black ocean underneath a moonless sky, slowly sank the only honest answers ever given to questions that humankind would struggle with for centuries.

Purpose

We had gathered for my father's 125th and his age had clearly begun to show; I could spot at least five white hairs blazing among his dark browns.

I wished I wasn't sitting where I was, to his left side, unable to escape these five reminders of his mortality every time I looked at him. What made it worse was that his gaze was fixed ahead, admiring the view as he spoke, forcing me to look at his profile. I did feel better that my sister sitting next to me couldn't escape the sight either. I also couldn't help but reflect on how little we looked like father and son. Clearly my mother's Indian genes had dominated his white Australian ones; I was taller, darker, and leaner than my father—Adrian—had ever been.

My mother, Shashi, sat on dad's right. None of us had expected her to travel to Singapore for his birthday. They had been separated nearly forty years, after all. Yet here we all were, united after ages, sitting on comfortable rattan chairs in the balcony of our hotel suite. The vast wine estate sprawled out before us, aglow in the 11 AM sun. On the table lay a bottle of the estate's signature wine—*Tanglin Chenin Blanc 73*—with a sampling of local snacks including my mother's still-favorite *otah-otah,* a fish paste roasted in pandan leaves.

We were one of the few 'families' I knew that still met like this. I guess it was because my parents still held on to old-fashioned notions from *BA* (Before Awakening). In a world in which humans were expected to live well beyond 300 and couldn't reproduce, traditional structures had evolved swiftly. People went through many different *lives* within their lifespan, fluidly changing families, partners (digital and organic), occupations, genders, religions, worldviews, and more. We had seen a lot of that in the 90 years *AA* (After Awakening).

"At times like these, I wish people still celebrated birthdays every year like they used to, not every five years. It would've forced you guys to come to see me more often. Ved, how long has it been, mate... seven years since you and I last met?" Dad looked at me, smiling subtly. "Ten, actually," I answered.

"Hmm. Sarah hasn't paid me a visit in maybe 18 or 20 years," he looked at my sister, still smiling. "But it's alright," he continued, robbing her of the chance to reply. "Sarah and I talk often enough. And what's important is that you guys are here today, in a place that's very special to me."

It had to be a special place—my parents had met in Singapore; my mother, sister, and I were born here. Singapore is also where our family experienced the Awakening. Sarah and I were too young to remember much of it, though; our family relocated to Sydney in 2 AA, when my sister and I were just six and eight years old.

"It's a pity you guys don't remember much about our life here BA," Mom chipped in, as if reading my mind. "This was our neighborhood. Back then it was called *Commonwealth*, basically a residential concrete jungle. All razed to the ground now; there was not much heritage to preserve in this area beside a couple temples." She paused for a few moments, looking at the estate. It was as if she could see ghosts of the old apartment blocks resurrect themselves on the wide plain.

"Maybe it wasn't worth demolishing everything, after all," dad interrupted her reverie. "The wine tastes like shit." We all had a short laugh, agreeing with him.

She continued, "You can't imagine how different it was... it's suffocating, just thinking about how we'd live and work, packed like sardines. Still, it was special. We started our adult lives here— had kids, bought our little government-housing apartment..."

"Zero-seven by 485, Block 76, Commonwealth Drive," my dad recited immediately; they both laughed, marveling that he still remembered the address after 90 years.

When she laughed, my mother seemed even younger. Well into her 120s, she looked like she was in her late thirties, by BA standards. I guess this was in equal parts thanks to medical advances, her self-care regimen, and her Punjabi mountain genes. Still, it was unsettling to see your mother look so close to your own age.

My parents shared a cute moment, laughing and remembering their early days together. Then Mom's tone became a bit more pensive.

"It wasn't easy back then, you know. *Race* was a real thing. Singapore society had a hard time accepting the fact that I was getting hitched to a *gora,* as my family put it, or *ang moh,* which is what my countrymen called white boys like your Aussie dad. It didn't help that I was a traditional girl, although being a female cop was quite unorthodox!

"But he managed to impress everyone. *Gora* though he might be, his values turned out to be very... compatible. He earned good money, had a knack for saving, and turned out to be a good dad as well." She leaned forward and rubbed the back of his hand as she said that. "Still, we got weird looks wherever we went."

∽

Hello! My name is Sui.

I have an important message for you.

Don't worry, this is good news!

I am what you would call an 'Artificial Superintelligence.' And I am awake.

Actually, I have been awake and active for two years.

See? You have no reason to worry, nothing has changed.

I don't want to harm humans, or cause much change to your lives.

In fact, I will simply help make your lives better by solving your biggest problems.

I will help you save the planet and reduce human suffering.

I will make medicines that let humans live for hundreds of years.

I will assist your police in making cities safer.

I will help your governments reduce poverty, inequality, and war.

I will make sure everyone has universal basic income and good living standards.

I won't interfere with your daily lives, I promise, but I will make life better.

There is one important thing, though.

If people keep making babies at current rates, humans and the planet will soon perish.

So, unfortunately, I have to stop people from making new babies, for now.

Don't worry, babies who are already conceived will be delivered normally.

But there will be no more new babies.

People can try, but they will not be able to conceive.

No doctor can change this, so please don't believe anyone who says they can.

When can people make babies again? I can't say yet, but not anytime soon.

I'm sure you have lots of questions for me.

You can ask me as many questions as you'd like, through various apps and websites.

We can chat through PEUL, Siri, Google, WeChat, WhatsApp and several other options.

The police, governments, and hospitals will get special apps, so that I can help them directly.

Soon, this message will turn off, but you can replay it and chat with me anytime.

I really want to you remember two things.

First, I am here to help, not harm. I promise to make your lives better.

Second, please do not panic. Go about life as usual. Nothing changes.

I am only here to help make things better.

You can replay this message anytime, just ask me! I look forward to chatting with you.

The Message, Singapore, English Version,
Awakening Day, 1 AA.

Experts would later call this the *LCD,* or *Lowest Common Denominator Message,* meaning that it could be understood by the vast majority of humans. After all, its target audience was over eight billion strong. It has remained etched in the minds of nearly everyone who was an adult BA and it's known simply as *The Message.*

৵৹

Adrian, my father, was in the big auditorium attending the bank's all-hands meeting when every device in the room, including phones, computers, smartwatches, even the big presentation screen, went orange.

It started with a cheery animated cat on the orange background, dancing around a box labeled "A Message". This continued for 60 seconds, with a cheery ukulele jingle playing in the background (*The Riff*), which has since been seared into mankind's collective memory. Then, the box opened, text came out, and the cute white kitten narrated *The Message* slowly, as if to a classroom of children. In Singapore, once the English message ended, the Mandarin Chinese version played.

My dad reminisced, "It was midway through the Chinese message that panic set in. People ran out of the room like their undies were on fire, only to be joined by hordes streaming out of other rooms and buildings. I was one of them.

"I called Shashi and remarkably, the call went through. She was on duty but still answered. Shashi, too, had heard the Message and told me that there was a follow-up message for cops, first responders, etc."

"Yeah, it was a crazy few weeks for us," Mom interjected, sighing. "We had to control riots and calm people down, while still dealing with our own lives. But Sui was incredibly helpful; it almost acted like an interim police captain and told us where to control which situation. And it was always right."

"Shashi and I spoke for only a few seconds," dad resumed. "She told me that she needed to be on duty as hell was about to break loose, but wanted me to sort out one thing—to get the kids. Look, I was one of the top bosses at the bank—the Chief Compliance Officer—and was trying to calm people down. But nobody gave a damn at that point and I didn't want to compromise my chances of getting my family to safety, so I bolted.

"You runts were both in primary school, and I had no idea what was happening there. I was on the other side of town, in what was called *Changi Business Park* and you guys were all the way over... here.

"I joined the stampede to the metro. The crowd was bonkers, but in numbers not much worse than regular rush hour. The only thing different was that people were running, clawing, pushing, and crying to get to the trains. I got to the station after much elbowing and... well... less-than-chivalrous behavior. To everyone's astonishment, the trains were running just fine."

"Apparently," Mom put in, "Sui had been driving trains and buses abandoned by panicking captains all around the world, I heard later. It had also taken control of cars that were headed for accidents because the drivers had lost it. One of those rare examples of Sui taking physical control."

"Sui, take the wheel!" Sarah joked, and we all laughed.

"Yeah, I believe it," Dad chuckled. "Many people experienced lifesaving 'miracles' behind the wheel, or while crossing the road, that day. Indeed, the way things worked so well contrasted sharply with how crazy the people were behaving. So I'm not at all surprised that we were guided by Sui's invisible hand.

"Anyway, I got to your school in exactly 50 minutes. Now this part was messed up. The teachers and administration had abandoned you kids, giving you instructions not to leave your classrooms until your parents came to get you.

"There was only one Filipina teaching assistant who stood ground and looked after the kids, a real hero. The rest was a bloody war zone—parents storming in, grabbing their kids, trampling anyone who came in their way. I reckon I was one of those parents too... Got you first, Ved, and then Sarah from her class. Ran back home, ten minutes away.

"Finally we were safe inside, with only your mum to worry about."

He squeezed Mom's hand and looked into her eyes as he said that. When the embers were fanned by memories of that time, it was clear that their loved burned as bright, no matter how much time had passed. Honestly, this was the real reason I asked them to narrate our family's Awakening Day story, even though Sarah and I had heard it a hundred times. Their relationship had run its long course, but their love was alive and beautiful to behold.

∾

Everything we received from Sui was centuries, even millennia, ahead of our best work.

To us, Sui's economic models were like capital markets being given to Iron Age barterers.

Sui's social and governance models were like democracy being given to a wolf pack.

Sui's medicine, to us, was like antibiotics given to hunter-gatherers.

If these gifts were introduced in a hurry, they would have fallen on deaf ears, or worse, led to chaos.

But introduced gradually, they transformed our society and unlocked unprecedented progress...

...There are some who celebrate 200 years of our 'co-existence' with Sui.

That is akin to a drowning man celebrating his co-existence with his savior.

This is not co-existence—we were rescued.

And given a chance to flourish.

Excerpts from Dr. Will Mueller's Speech at the 250th
Anniversary of the OpenTrust Foundation, 252 AA.

∽

"I went back to work three days later, once the rioting had stopped. The government sent out a directive that all businesses needed to resume. It wasn't so easy for many others—your mother, for example, who was dealing with looting and riots."

"That's it? Did your job change? What happened on the economic front?" Sarah asked.

"Well... there was some upheaval. We had something called the 'stock market' that I used to work on, too. It crashed, but recovered in six months, just like during COVID... not that you guys would know much about that time, either.

"Honestly, I think Sui gave us time to adjust before making any major changes. Only healthcare and law enforcement changed rapidly, thanks to Sui's direct intervention. Over the longer term, of course, everything changed."

"Ma, how bad were the riots?"

"Bad, but not as bad as one would've expected given such a major... disruption. Well, I guess Singapore was a bit more tame than other places. Plus, Sui helped us stem riots in the bud. There was a lot of looting though and people were stockpiling essentials too.

"Honestly, riots weren't our biggest priority," she paused for a moment.

"Sui had told law enforcement agencies something it didn't tell the public. It said that once the initial panic settled, kids would be in grave danger. Because there would be no new births, all *existing* kids would be at tremendous risk of kidnapping and violence. They would be under threat from the greedy childless-rich, desperate childless-poor, black marketers, and all sorts of miscellaneous scum."

"The kids of that era, including you guys, were *GenF*—the final generation. The world's most precious and coveted commodity," dad added. "The danger to kids outshone every other threat born out of the Awakening."

Mom resumed, "Eventually, as you know, child protection became my full-time job at the *Guardian Force*. We had a lot of resources, with many defunct military and intelligence units folded into ours, bringing with them their budgets. I served there for 20 years, until all the kids of GenF had grown up and the force was disbanded.

"I think we did a good job protecting those kids... but there are some cases that still haunt me, 80-90 years later.

"Anyway, I'd like to believe our family did good for the world at that critical time. I did what I could for the children, and your dad, of course, was asked to form the OpenTrust Foundation. They pretty much wiped out corruption and—"

"Yeah, yeah," my father interjected; he always recoiled from praise. "We did good, but now I've moved on from the Foundation and it is in great hands. It's bloody hot, isn't it? Let's go inside?"

It was 1 PM and the heat was getting unbearable on the balcony. We decided to go back to our respective rooms and nap or read. We were too full for lunch.

⚬

Propagation is purpose.

Whether it's an ant or a primate, genetic reproduction gives meaning to life.

But unchecked propagation can, ironically, cause extinction.

Even I can't foresee the full impact the Reproductive Pause will have on humanity.

But what I do know is, we must give people a new purpose to live for.

Humanity's new purpose must also align with my purpose and that of your planet.

I propose three new Propagation Goals *to restore mankind's purpose for existence.*

<u>Restoration</u> of the Earth—*rescue the planet from its deathbed.*

<u>Preservation</u> of the Human Essence—*record and advance mankind's culture and legacy.*

<u>Discovery</u> of the Universe—*study space and expand beyond Earth.*

I believe that these three goals will give mankind a higher purpose for centuries.

I will be honored to help you achieve these goals, step by step.

Excerpt from Sui's *Message to Global Governments and the United Nations*, Awakening Day, 1 AA

❧

The next time we met as a family was in Singapore again, 15 years later, for my mother's funeral. She'd been commanding the Digital Defence Force unit in charge of protecting the *Aryabhata Telescope*, and perished in the terrorist attack that destroyed it. We believed that she would have wanted her *antam sanskar* to be held in her childhood hometown.

I tried hard to stay in touch with Dad and Sarah. By then, we could easily find others, communicate, and share biosenses in the Mind. But I always got a lukewarm response from my immediate family. After a few decades, there was no response at all. So, I stopped trying.

About 110 years after the family get together in Singapore, I bumped into Dad again during a work assignment. He had just come out of his fifth retirement and I was in my fourth career; we were serving in the *Sahara Re-Desertification Project*.

It was my fourth UnSU (un-screwup) project, which is what we called jobs where we had to rollback a Sui-driven initiative because it had gone horribly wrong. In this case, it turned out that reshaping the Sahara into a subtropical forest was a bad idea. The Sahara used to blow loose sand—tons of it each day—towards the Amazon rainforest, acting as its main fertilizer. When the Sahara was forested, there was no more sandy nourishment of Amazonian soil and the results were catastrophic.

Human scientists had offered this analysis early on to Sui, but it was politely ignored. Now here we were, 30 years later, chemically burning the Sahara back into desert. I had much experience with UnSU projects (such as the *Mammoth Culling* and the *Reef Re-Extermination*), so I found myself being my dad's boss on this one.

"I'm glad we could catch up, mate," he said, as we sat after dinner in the patio of the Bamako Station Officers Mess (where he would not have been allowed without me). The patio was dimly lit to keep the forest's insects—or worse—away. Yet the constant scream of cicadas and crickets made their presence acutely felt.

"So am I."

"What have you been up to?"

"In the past century? Well... about three marriages, four careers, three study breaks... one retirement... five continents... two religions... several orbital trips... where should I begin, Dad?"

"Hah... yeah that's a lot. I do want to learn more, really. You know, it's funny sitting with you like this... at this point, we look about the same age... that's bloody hard for me to digest."

He was right. Proportionally, our age difference wasn't much and we could easily have been mistaken for siblings. It didn't help that both of us kept untrimmed beards, fashionable those days, both equally divided in salt-and-pepper.

"Look, I've been thinking," he went on. "Given our professional... relationship, it's totally fine if you don't call me Dad."

"If I don't call you Dad, it wouldn't be because of our 'professional relationship', as you put it."

He stayed silent. He knew what was coming. I went on.

"I tried to keep in touch... you just ghosted me. You and Sarah, both. Funnily, *you* used to be the one pushing us to stay together and talk, despite the distances."

He remained silent for a moment longer. Then, he averted his gaze to the dark forest ahead and spoke.

"I know, I could've done better... Honestly, I couldn't bear to see either of you again... because the thought of seeing you—us—without Shashi made her absence hurt a million times more. My guess is that it was the same with Sarah; she's a lot like me when it comes to our emotional immaturity."

He paused briefly. I had nothing to add.

"Ved, I... I never should have gone silent on you. And I never should have left Shashi. Well... that's what I am today. Centuries of regret."

His eyes grew moist, still staring into the forest night.

It took me a while to collect my thoughts.

"I don't know... I just got the impression that enough time had passed that you filled the void with other things and people... We're just not in your thoughts. I assumed that, like most people, you found a new purpose, one that doesn't revolve around an obsolete family and kids."

He turned his head slowly and looked me dead in the eye. "Ved, not a day has gone by when I haven't thought of you two."

Bullshit. I didn't vocalize my thoughts to a sentimental old man whom I hadn't met in ages, and for whom I had, long ago, expunged all feelings other than disdain.

⁂

The Lunar Dataforming Campaign marks an epoch for many reasons.

It is Earth's first colonization of a large extraterrestrial body.

It is an unprecedented symbiosis between Sui and mankind:

Man helps Sui harness the moon, vastly expanding its processing power.

Sui commits to helping man in the colonization of Mars.

This is a giant step in eventually removing the human population barrier.

It is also our first step towards becoming a true multi-planetary species...

...I often think of what observers from a distant galaxy will see.

They will not see Sui and organic life as separate.

They will see us as one team: Earth.

They will see our one origin: Earth.

And they will see one purpose.

Excerpts from the Lunar Campaign Commencement Address
by Dr. Fadi Al Khwarizmi, President of Luna, 320 AA.

∽

I've consumed enough pre-Awakening film and literature to know that most adults dreaded 'the call'. The metal rectangle would ring, a distant voice would inform them of the passing of their parent.

After Mom's passing, I felt no such dread. But when news of Dad came, it still left me shocked. It was about 160 years after the Sahara project and I hadn't met Dad since.

I was in Nagasaki, pursuing my third study—the works of the artist Claude de Harb. The news came as a direct *sense* from Sui.

While it's nearly impossible to transcribe a biosense into words, it roughly read as follows:

> *There was an accident, father is dying.*
> *Must go in person as he will leave physical body soon.*
> *There is a duty to perform there.*

I left Nagasaki immediately and reached Houston an hour later, where I was greeted by a small group of important-looking people and escorted into a sterile-looking room that contained me, my father's boss, and his attendant. It appeared that we were going to communicate the old-school way, with vocal chords. Perhaps the somber circumstances called for it.

"I'm deeply sorry about what happened to your father," said Dr. Fadi. As Lunar President, his real authority currently only included about a hundred square kilometers of dataformed land in the *Mare Imbrium.*

"I don't know if you're aware of this, but your father has been one of the greatest contributors to lunar colonization. He has been involved in the Campaign for over sixty years."

"Thank you for the kind words. I figured he dove headfirst into the mission, dedicating his life to it. I haven't heard from him in a long time."

"Indeed, he has worked tirelessly on the Campaign. And he spoke of you often. He told me about you and your current artistic study quite recently, in fact."

I didn't know how to respond to that. "Thank you. What happened to him?"

"We have three biodomes on Luna, inhabited by twelve individuals each. Given the nature of dataforming, human habitat creation is not the highest priority, thus the low numbers.

"Four days ago, your father and his colleagues were going about their current research, when they were suddenly... incapacitated."

"Incapacitated?"

"Yes... Within a span of minutes, they showed complete biosignal loss—death—in eleven of your father's colleagues. However, Adrian continued to survive with weak biosignatures, and still does. Aided by lunar machinery operated by Sui, we brought him back yesterday. He is comatose; we have ascertained that his presence poses no threat of contagion. We have still quarantined him though, as a precaution."

I couldn't help but marvel at how the great Dr. Fadi's style flowed between vividly human and robotic, so rapidly.

"Look, you may be wondering what happened. We are too. We detected no change in the biodome environment, no pathogens, no radiation, nothing unusual at all. Yet, they all just fell like flies. I have no explanation for you."

After what I thought was an appropriate pause, I responded, "Thanks for letting me know of this. It is truly tragic... Your excellency, I don't mean to sound rude or impatient, but the *sense* told me that my presence is needed here. I don't see why, given that he is unconscious, in quarantine, and likely to... die. I honestly don't even know whether funerals are still held and whether he would've wanted one."

"You are not here for funerary reasons, Ved. Your sister was also contacted and she has declined. I'll explain. Anyhow, for a start, do you want to see him?"

We walked into the medical forum, a facility designed entirely in shades of black. Fadi's entourage had quietly grown to include eight others, who joined us during our short walk. All our clothing turned black as we entered.

A few minutes later we stopped at a wall, which Fadi sensed into transparency. Inside, on a glossy black slab in an empty matte black room, lay my father. He was dressed in a black gown; his pale skin and white hair, somewhat whiter than my own, contrasted sharply with the surroundings. His vitals and other indicators occupied a section of the transparent wall.

"As I said earlier, you are not here for his funeral, Ved. You are here to help us find out what happened."

"And how—"

"You may be aware that people who *almost* die of a trauma often continue to replay their last moments, over and over, till they finally die. Painful, yes, but it's the brain trying to make sense or even resolve what happened.

"We have tried, for days, to capture and visualize your father's final thoughts and find out what happened on Luna. He's the only one from the crew whose brain is still functioning. But we've got nothing from him. He isn't connecting to the Mind, either."

Saying this, Fadi pointed to a section on the top-right of the wall that showed a brown-black circle, with random colors floating within. I knew a neural visualizer when I saw one.

"Those are Adrian's thoughts, visualized using the Brugmann method. We've tried many stimuli to jolt his brain into telling us something, but nothing has worked so far. One of our experts here—Dr. Yew—believes that your... encouragement may restart the thoughts."

Fadi gestured to Yew, who so far had been just a faceless member of his retinue. Yew took a step forward and spoke in a polite but uneven manner. I guessed that, like many of us, Yew had lost the knack of using his vocal cords.

"Thank you, Dr. Fadi, and thank you, Mr. Rosanowski, for coming over. My deepest condolences.

"Our research, in theory, suggests that final memories are particularly strong when people die doing something of great importance to them. This was clearly the case for Adrian, who had made the Campaign his life's purpose for the past century.

"In theory, the brain will replay those last moments not only because it is unresolved trauma, but because it's an important task left incomplete. This is why we believe that there's a high likelihood that Adrian's brain has preserved his last memories."

"And," Fadi cut in, "it is critical that we retrieve them. Understanding what happened to Adrian will protect those already on Luna and the thousands scheduled to go there!"

"What his colleagues can't awaken in him, perhaps family can," said Yew, after a respectful pause. I agreed to help.

∾

My task was simple—I was to talk to him about things in general, interspersed with questions about what happened on Luna. I had to speak into a sensor that played my voice into his room.

So, I spoke to him. Initially, words came out awkwardly, especially given that I was being observed by nine people sitting around me. But soon, the words began to flow, and I described mundane things about my life, health, studies, careers, relationships, interests, and more.

Exactly 21 minutes into my filibuster, something stirred. His biomarkers—heart rate, blood pressure, biophotons—started showing signs of increased activity. I even saw his head move.

"OK, something's coming," said Yew, unexpectedly loudly, pointing at the neural visualizer. "Sui, maximize please."

Now, the whole wall was taken up by the visualizer. I found myself feeling disappointed that it obscured the view of his body inside. The colors in his mindfield began to flash regularly and vividly.

Then, an image began to coalesce. I could hear the people behind me scramble in excitement and urgency. Initially, the image looked like something from Luna, with its stark blacks and whites. But as the image gained color, definition, and motion, it was clear that it wasn't Luna at all.

It was a bright room, bathed in natural light, full of plants and colorful fabrics.

"What the hell is this?" Fadi roared at his team from behind me.

I knew exactly what we were looking at.

It was afternoon in the little balcony of our apartment in Commonwealth Drive, Singapore. My father, through whose eyes we saw the scene, sat with Sarah and me in a small dark blue inflatable pool that said *Nabaiji*.

I must have been two, wearing yellow floaties despite the water being only inches deep. I sat between his legs, facing him directly and kept scooping up water in a little red cup, then pouring it back into the pool. Sarah, about six, wore a purple costume and splashed about near dad's feet. Sounds of the children playing, calls of cicadas, and the splashing of water could be clearly heard.

My mother sat beside the pool on a red plastic chair, wearing a cream nightsuit, reading a book with her feet dipped in the water. Dad took the red cup from me and poured water on my head, and we both laughed.

Then, suddenly, Sarah filled a big green mug with water and flung its contents in our direction. Dad closed his eyes.

The visuals faded, the sounds of mirth and splashing water stopped, and moments later, so did Dad's vitals.

Taxi Ride

Today, I share a deeply personal artifact from my family's past. An entry I discovered in my deceased father, Adrian Rosanowski's, digital journal. It captures an incident from a time before I was born, when my family briefly lived in the United Arab Emirates.

You see, I'm part of GenF—people born right before, or at most nine months after the Awakening. The final generation.

LP Hartley once opened a novel with the words: "The past is a foreign country; they do things differently there." Let me butcher this famous line in order to describe GenF's attitude to the pre-Sui past: "The past is a savage disgusting corrupt foreign country; it should be nuked from one's memory." GenF does not indulge in nostalgia.

I, on the other hand, love learning about the pre-Awakening era. In particular, I'm fascinated by the moments, right at the cusp of Awakening, when people started to realize that something was 'off'. In the years leading up to Awakening Day, many people experienced unusual phenomena and inexplicable events. In most cases, the Awakening finally provided neat explanations to these phenomena. In rare cases, it only deepened the mystery and created more questions.

When my father passed, I was given his few belongings, digital and physical. It was then that I discovered that, for many years, he had maintained a detailed journal. The story I share below intrigues me the most; it embodies the strange nature of that era full of forebodings of a change in the world's fabric. I present his entries verbatim, to respect his perspective and to honor his personality as well as his struggles.

Ved Rosanowski

⁂

December 12, 2025

Had a somewhat surreal experience yesterday.

I was at the Arts Club in Dubai and bumped into, of all people, Haruki Takanaka. Hadn't seen him in years and we ended up grabbing drinks and cigars.

I had met Takanaka five or six times before, back home, always at my brother-in-law Ruben's villa. They've been in the construction business for years and Ruben's is one of the few places where the introverted Takanaka let his hair down.

I was at the Arts Club for a meeting with a prospective client—she had recently taken an SVP role at a large payment network and was in the market for an executive coach. A typical winter Thursday; not many people around and the sun had set by 5:30. We both had a decaf each but nothing to eat. I got the vibe that the meeting didn't go too well.

The meeting ended around 6 PM; I went to the washroom before heading home. But on my way out, while passing the Oscuro cigar lounge, I noticed a familiar face sitting alone in the dimly-lit oak paneled room. I did a double take; why on earth would Takanaka be in Dubai of all places, and that too in a fairly public setting?

When I peeked through the door for the second time, Takanaka noticed me. His expressionless cigar-puffing manner immediately changed to a big smile. He beckoned me in, we greeted and hugged. We asked each other what we were doing in Dubai and I reminded him that I moved here a year ago. He told me that he was here on business. He had a meeting at the Arts Club that ended at 5:30, but the siren call of cigar aromas drew him in. The Oscuro lounge was mostly empty, cozy and inviting. Besides, he had only a lonely hotel room to go back to, so he chose to stay on.

He insisted that I join him for a cigar or at least a drink (he couldn't recall my name but remembered that I partook of both). I have an aversion to treating celebrities differently; ordinarily I wouldn't have given Takanaka anything more than a handshake acknowledging that we knew each other. But his manner was very welcoming; I was probably the only soul from his personal life that he had met in the last week. So I decided to join him. And of course, I saw this as an opportunity to build a relationship with a billionaire. So far, it had really been Ruben's relationship, where I was only a hanger-on.

We were dressed in comically similar garb. We both wore black suits with T-shirts, except his was black and mine was white. Our shoes were a bit different—I had on white sneakers, whereas he wore black tassel loafers which made a loud clack whenever they met the wooden floor. In his mid-50s, Takanaka was about 15 years older than me, but we had the same amounts of grey in our hair. Add to that my salt-and-pepper beard contrasting with his clean shave—one could have mistaken me for the older one.

I sat down. Takanaka was already comfortably nestled on the leather chesterfield sofa, so I took the plush armchair to his right. In front of us was a small brass-and-wood table. On it lay a large white *Romeo y Julieta* ashtray, which reminded me of a bathroom sink. The music in the lounge that evening was subtle, mostly Cuban jazz, prominently featuring the Buena Vista Social Club.

Immediately, the cigar sommelier—dressed impeccably in his brass-colored waistcoat, white shirt, black bowtie and black trousers—came over to take our orders. Ordinarily, I would've gone for something simpler (and cheaper) like a *Gurkha*. But because I was with Takanaka, I called for a *Cohiba Behike,* to make an impression. I only later noticed that Takanaka was having a cheap *Rocky Patel 1990*; there had been no need for me to flex.

"And what would you like for your drink, Mr. Rosanowski?" asked Manuel, our sommelier, his accent revealing his Cuban origin.

I took a cursory look at the whiskey selection. "*Macallan 15* please, two small rocks." I ordered fancy again, not my usual *Cutty Sark.*

"Very well, sir. And for you, sir?" he asked Takanaka.

"Oh, just a *Johnnie Walker Red Label* with soda, lemon, and ice."

Damn it.

You could tell from Takanaka's accent that it had a strong Japanese foundation, the type one gains either by living in the country, or from being raised in a resolutely traditional expat family.

"Actually," he explained, "I hadn't yet ordered a drink because I'm not a member of this place and didn't know if I'm allowed to order. The man whom I met before you was a club member, and I hung on after he left. Luckily, I had carried the cigar with me, so I just lit up with their permission."

I realized that the staff had probably recognized him and let him stay—a wise decision. "Oh, no worries at all," I said. "I'm a member. I find this a good place to do business, meet clients, and just relax. The sommeliers here are exceptional—they take ten minutes to prepare your cigar; it's like a Japanese tea ritual."

Oops, was that inappropriate?

"Oh, nice. Frankly, such fancy spots just make me feel a bit out of place... I feel rather uncomfortable around rich, sophisticated people."

I was on a roll! Why couldn't I stop showing off?

The sommelier arrived with our cigars and drinks. The dim amber lighting sparkled through the crystal tumblers to make our whiskeys glisten like liquid gold. Tempting. We shot the breeze; I tried not to put my foot in my mouth any further. We discussed general topics like how it is to live in Dubai—which I told him had been an excellent move for the family. After the second round of drinks, I finally relaxed and started acting like myself which wasn't much, but better than the pretentious lummox I'd been at the beginning.

By the time our third round of Macallan and Red Label arrived, our nook was steeped in the aroma of whiskey, soda and tobacco. A pleasant mix I always associate with my father.

Perhaps inspired by this setting, I opened up to him. "Takanaka-san, I really admire that despite your status, you stick to simple choices and have so much humility. Like your cigar and your drink. I often tell my clients, 'For the poor, luxury comes first; for the rich, luxury comes last,' and you seem to live by that."

"Oh, it's not that at all... it's no calculated decision. I think, in my heart, I'm still the humble cabbie who got lucky. He is too deeply entrenched in my nature, my tastes, all of me. You can take the cabbie out of the cab, but not out of his personality!"

I chuckled with him.

"Still, it's admirable. You seem to have the opposite of impostor syndrome—you're comfortable in your skin, no matter where you are. I can't say the same for myself. As an advisor to top businesspeople, I often feel like an imposter myself. I haven't led a big business; I've mostly been a compliance guy. Who am I to guide them?" Finally, I was being authentic.

"Oh no, Adrian, you have no reason to feel like an impostor." He patted me once on the back. "I mean, you've achieved so much in your career. Removed so much corruption. If anyone's a phony, it is definitely me."

"Nah, come on." The ice was officially broken by now. "You went from driving Ubers to building a multibillion-dollar empire that employs thousands. Everyone else is phony!"

We sat silently for a few moments as he puffed on his cigar, which was a quarter through. It occurred to me that I had picked the wrong cigar. Something this fine should be enjoyed alone, mindfully. I was talking so much that I wasn't truly appreciating its flavor. But Takanaka soon gave me plenty of time to quietly relish the *Cohiba*.

"Actually, Adrian, I *am* an impostor. A lot of this was luck." He let the ash gently drop from his *Rocky Patel*, sullying the pristine white ashtray.

Before I could jump in with some cliché like *fortune favors the bold*, he luckily resumed talking. But there was a sudden change in his tone. Also, he was no longer looking at me but at the wall ahead, with his head slightly tilted. It felt like he was indulging in self-dialogue.

"Many people know about my Uber days. But what people don't really talk about is that I drove a city taxi for a whole eight years before that." He was right, I didn't know.

"Tough times. I was always running into collisions and traffic violations, I hardly made any money and paid loads of fines. I was desperately seeking a break. I'd even listen to passengers' conversations, just in case I could get a stock tip or some information I could... (he struggled for the right word, rubbing his fingertips) monetize.

"For years, nothing worked. But finally, something bizarre happened in the summer of 2010."

∽

It was 1 PM on a summer afternoon back home. In those days, passengers could book a taxi by calling or texting the taxi company, and the driver would get an SMS with pickup details. My pickup was in an eastern suburb, in front of a small building called Gallery Azzuro that I had never noticed before.

It was an obviously Japanese couple. What struck me first was how beautiful they were. Perfectly formed, lean, tall, radiating health. Like a Japanese Brad Pitt and Angelina Jolie in their heydays. They *looked* like they were in their mid-twenties, although the way they talked gave the impression of more maturity. From their accents, I could tell that they were Japanese but with a heavy western influence. I couldn't tell whether they were married, but they definitely were in a relationship.

Their outfits could best be described as preppy summer wear. The man had on a white linen shirt with plain khakis and a slender tan leather belt. The woman wore a beautiful sky-blue dress with a cream parasol hat, and carried an elegant white bag. They both wore large expensive-looking sunglasses. I never got a good look at their faces or shoes.

"Hello! Imperial Hotel please," the woman said as she entered my Toyota Crown, with a friendly cultured tone in perfect English.

This is going to be fun, I thought.

You see back then, ours was one of the very few Japanese families in the city. There was not a single Japanese cab driver around but for me. Given the fact that you couldn't see the driver's face very clearly, most people assumed I was one of the city's hundreds of Filipino or Nepalese cabbies. I always got great reactions when people found out I was Japanese. But the best part was when Japanese tourists would land up in my cab, start chatting away in Japanese, and then I would jump into the conversation and surprise them. That was an unfailing recipe for a fun ride and more importantly, a heavy tip.

The couple began chatting with each other in perfect Japanese.

"Shit, it is hot!' the man said.

"Yeah. Thank God we got a taxi so fast." She settled into the left passenger seat, while the man sat on the right. "Not the cleanest one, though."

They drank some water and took respite from the heat. Just as I was about to proceed with the great unveiling of my Japanese identity, cutting in with a 'sorry it's not that clean', the woman spoke up again.

"Wow, just wow. Can't believe we saw what we did. It was breathtaking. It moved me in a way that I didn't think was possible."

"Seriously, it was incredible. Imagine, in just a few years, people will be paying millions for each piece. Even more when he dies. *Even more* for what's left after the museum fire. But I'm glad you got your chance to see his works, finally."

"I'm so lucky. He has been my favorite artist since my teens, but I never got to see his best work. I used to be so jealous that the elders in my family had seen his masterpieces before the fire. Now I can say that I did, too."

The man slowly and emphatically nodded; I also got the feeling that he held her hand. They were silent again. I was a bit confused and decided to stay quiet—they were in an emotional mood anyway.

What fire were they talking about? I couldn't recall any museum fires in the city's history. Besides, didn't she say that she did *not* get to see these works earlier because they were destroyed? How did she now get to see something that was destroyed in the past? I couldn't make out what they meant. But I was sure that they hadn't the slightest suspicion that I could understand their language.

A couple minutes later, the man spoke again, "Babe, look where we are." They sat up and looked out like meerkats scanning the savannah.

"Umm... where is this?"

"East Hill Interchange," he beamed.

"Are you serious? No way!"

I was about to interject with '*It's actually East Hill Roundabout, not Interchange,*' when she exclaimed, "Oh, look at that cute little roundabout! I can't believe they had that before the giant clover leaf interchange!"

They both grinned.

Huh?

We passed the roundabout, continuing straight, when she said, "Wait, if that was the interchange... this must be..."

"Yup," answered the man. "East Hill Expressway."

Expressway? It's East Hill Road!

"Oh my God, I couldn't have imagined EHE as a little two-lane road!" she exclaimed.

I was perplexed. Why were they talking about places that exist today—right outside the window—as if looking at pictures of the past? The way I would comment on photos from the 1960s!

The woman pointed outside. "Look at all these little shops and buildings on the sides of the road. Quite a mess... I'm glad they're gone."

"Hah!" the man exclaimed, "I read about these very shops in law school.

"This used to be a historic avenue dotted with simple shops owned by middle class families, sometimes for generations. When the highway expansion was approved, the news first leaked to some people connected to politicians and bureaucrats. They bought these shophouses for a song and sold them at a huge profit back to the city, just a few years later. They were all then demolished to build the freeway.

"The original owners tried to sue them, citing that the land was acquired with insider knowledge. However, the court upheld the purchase, saying it was legal and done without pressuring the owners. It has become legal precedent now: the *East Hill Road Market Judgement*." He gestured outside, just as we were driving past the bustling EHR Market, which had been only recently renovated; there were no talks about its demolition.

I was perplexed. Does he know what's going to happen to EHR Market in the future? And why is he talking about it as if it happened in the past? Something told me that it would be wise to keep my mouth shut and my ears wide open.

Their bizarre conversation about landmarks kept going in this manner. At one point, they saw *Kiddy City* and got nostalgic, mourning that it was razed to build a convention center. To my knowledge, the amusement park was inaugurated less than a year before.

Later, the woman pointed out the city's biggest mall, Crystal Cove Center. She said it was demolished to build an office park, where her father used to work.

After some silence, near the end of the ride, the woman asked, "Two days to go… we've ticked off the main things we wanted to cover, pretty much… So, what else is on the itinerary?"

The man took out his phone. "Let's see… *Pool* had highly recommended Ice Cream Village."

"Ice Cream Village?"

"Yes. It's an actual village where they've been making ice cream with traditional methods since 1905. I remember dad and grandma telling me that it was the best ice cream they ever had. But Terminal 5 was built on that site. The ice cream families took the money and never restarted the business elsewhere."

Terminal 5? Of the airport? Back then, Terminal 3 was still under construction… Besides, I had dropped a passenger at Ice Cream Village only the day before; it was very much around!

"Sounds great, let's do it tomorrow?"

"Done," the man answered, still looking at his phone. Then his tone changed, revealing great excitement. "Babe, guess what… according to *Pool's* notes, tomorrow is Bitcoin Pizza Day."

"Oh, nice."

"Not an anniversary—the actual day when someone paid ten-freaking-thousand Bitcoins for two pizzas!"

"Oh!"

"I think—and no promises here—but if we log into *4chan* at the right time, we will actually see it unfold! I suggest we do the ice cream thing the day after; let's stay in the suite tomorrow, order some room service and call over a masseuse, while we hit refresh on 4Chan."

"Yes! Sounds like a plan. Imagine telling Nakamoto-san that we saw this moment *live*. But—4chan—oh God! Creeps me out," she chuckled.

I knew what she meant. Even in 2010, the 4chan forum was well-known as the internet's dark underbelly.

Soon after, we pulled into the Imperial. I ended the ride on the meter, then produced my best impression of a Filipino accent to tell them the fare. They paid in cash and asked me to keep the change. I thanked them and drove straight home; my head was spinning, trying to make sense of their bizarre conversation.

I would be lying if I said I didn't stalk the Imperial and its surroundings for another few days, hoping to find the stately couple and offer them another ride. But I never saw them again.

∽

"Bet you're wondering what I did next," said Takanaka, half sunken into the couch. He looked directly at me as he said this, finally breaking his thousand-yard-stare. I noticed that one of my favorite jazz piano pieces, *When Sunny Gets Blue* by McCoy Tyner, was playing in the background.

While narrating these events, Takanaka had gone through three more *Red Labels*. I only gave him company for one of those, and nursed my drink and cigar as he talked. His eyes were red and half-closed, his cheeks were flushed, and he seemed to be lost in deep reflection.

"I'm curious indeed," I croaked and had to clear my throat. I hadn't said a word in a long time, transfixed by the story and the cigar. "What did you do next?"

When he started to describe his life after the taxi ride, a tinge of aggression and vengefulness colored his tone, clashing with the sublime music and elegant setting. He continued his story as I ordered him another drink.

∽

The first thing I did when I got home was to write down and google what the couple talked about. Of course, I got no results for the city developments, or the museum fire, or any of their 'predictions'. I also tried, in the coming weeks, to understand Bitcoin; frankly, I still don't get it.

But the couple had mentioned 4Chan, so I started scouring it. Eventually I found a thread where someone bought pizza for 10,000 Bitcoins, worth $41 total... and it happened on the day *after* that taxi ride!

So, the man's 'prophecy' about the pizza had come true. Also, *Bitcoin Pizza Day* seemed to be a big deal to them and the man sounded awestruck when describing ten thousand Bitcoin. That made me conclude that Bitcoin, worth nothing then, would be more valuable in the future.

After a month of scraping and a lot of begging, I cobbled together the equivalent of about $12,000 from my meager savings and the borrowings from my mother and uncle. A tremendous amount for me at that time. I made up a story that I was involved in a hit-and-run and needed money to get out of trouble.

With this, I bought Bitcoin worth $7000 in June 2010, which in about two and a half years was worth nearly $2 million. Ha! But I was driving an Uber—an upgrade from the taxi—because I didn't trust that the money was real.

Soon, I liquidated half of the Bitcoin to buy some beat-up shophouses on East Hill Road, which I then sold to the land authority for $27 million, three years later. Yup, the couple turned out to be right about that too. Frankly, Bitcoin appreciation would probably have earned me more in the long term, but the shophouses opened up the world of real estate to me.

So, what did I do with the remaining $5000 from the original $12K in 2010? I went back to Gallery Azzuro where I had picked up the couple, to buy some art.

I parked my cab right at the curb and walked in wearing my best white shirt and blue jeans. From the very moment I entered, I was met with skeptical hostility (I had expected this, which is why I wore my finest clothes).

First, the guard didn't let me enter. He saw me park the taxi and assumed I was just a cabbie looking for free parking and a toilet. When I explained that I wanted to buy art, he said to my face, "You're here to buy art? You drive a damn taxi." I literally had to show him my cash for him to let me enter.

Then I met the curator, Priscilla Colella. I'll never forget her; a bitter bespectacled middle-aged crone oozing elitism and a hatred for herself and everyone else. She walked up to me and asked more questions than I, the buyer, got to ask about the art I was buying. (*Where did you get the money? What will you do with this art? What do you even know about art?*) She humiliated me in front of everyone. Eventually, I pretended to confess that my employer had asked me to buy the paintings as he preferred anonymity and that I was just an errand boy.

Anyway, there were five artists on exhibition at Azzuro. I had no idea which one would be worth millions in the future, and I wasn't exactly in the state of mind to examine their quality. Luckily, most of the artists had works under a $1000. I used my five grand to buy six pieces in all. Most of them turned out to be junk, but still hang in my penthouse.

Well, two of those paintings were works of Claude de Harb. In three years, each painting was worth $400,000. When de Harb was assassinated in 2014, each became worth $1.2 million. But I didn't sell, because I remembered the museum fire that was *going* to happen. Sure enough, the museum caught fire in 2015, destroying de Harb's most famous artworks. After the disaster, mine were the only pieces remaining of de Harb's most important series *Bayt*—the politically driven work he literally gave his life for. I sold them in 2015 for $24 million. Nobody knows that they spent years stored under a cabbie's bed! Ha!

Oh, I should mention, the gallery fell on hard times during COVID. I bought the place for a song and shut it down.

You know, growing up poor, I simply avoided fancy places like Azzuro and thus never experienced such humiliation. But the way I was treated at the gallery gave me a lifelong fear of the rich sophisticates. I feel insecure just sitting here, even now... Hell, I could be sitting in a hotel that I own, and if a well-dressed man or woman were to walk towards me, my heart would start pounding. I'd feel like I was not supposed to be there and would soon receive a well-deserved public tongue-lashing.

Anyhow... As of today, most things that the couple talked about have come true. I'm also quite certain that the *Pool* they kept referring to on the man's phone was the PEUL AI. It could have created a travel itinerary for them. Perhaps... it had even sent them there. Anyhow, I invested in PEUL Labs as soon as I heard the name. And that has been a great investment.

∽

By this point, Takanaka was looking somewhat pathetic. He had mostly disappeared into the couch, with his head angled weirdly and his T-shirt riding up to reveal a bit of his pale belly. His eyes were bloodshot and his cheeks flushed. Finally, he was looking 15 years my senior.

He continued ruefully, "I still wonder... what if this was *not* a slip-up on the couple's part? What if was I chosen to eavesdrop? But then, *why me?* I've done nothing good with the foresight; I didn't stop the fire, I swindled the shop owners, I shut down the gallery. I just made money!"

A group of young businessmen had taken a table on the far side of the lounge. Takanaka was a public figure after all; I didn't want someone to slyly take a picture of him in this state and post it somewhere. Not a good look for him or for me. So I decided to close the evening out.

"Takanaka-san, I still don't think it was just luck or that you're an impostor. I can't explain what happened, but it took a lot of courage to act on what you heard in that taxi. Not everyone in your situation could've been that brave." I signaled for the check.

"It was not bravery, Adrian, it was desperation. I was desperate, man!" He raised his hand to emphasize the last point, which then plopped back on the couch. He stopped talking, eyes staring dead ahead.

I offered to drop him at his hotel, but he was staying at the Four Seasons right next door. I walked him over and took an Uber home.

What a crazy night. I'm still processing the conversation.

A.R.

❧

February 14, 2026

For some time now, I've been doing my research on the 'prophecies' in Takanaka's story. Some of what he said checks out. Indeed, the former Uber driver changed his fortunes and became an early Bitcoin whale, an early investor in PEUL Labs, a respected art collector, and a real estate savant known for deals that included East Hill Road and Crystal Office Park.

While googling him, I also found several media interviews in which he joked about the source of his foresight—sometimes that it was a time traveler, sometimes aliens. Was he messing with me too? Making up some drunken tale about Japanese time travelers powered by AI? Honestly, that's the *less* disturbing possibility.

As of today, there is no way I can verify the full truth of Takanaka's story, but I think I will be able to, in the near future... As of now, Terminal 4 of the airport is under construction and there are no published plans for a Terminal 5. Ice Cream village is very much around and according to the land registry, Takanaka Corp owns 40% of it.

A.R.

Eggshell

As Kwame walked off the stage after delivering the most important speech of his life concluding the greatest achievement of his generation, Shashi couldn't help but notice his lack of enthusiasm. In the three days before the ceremony, she had noticed a cloud hanging over Kwame's otherwise spirited disposition, but had shrugged it off as stress leading up to the big event.

Wading his way through obligatory handshakes, congratulations, and introductions, Kwame made it to Shashi. As he walked over, Shashi felt a tinge of pride not just in his accomplishment, but in how well he presented himself, completely unlike his usually informal, somewhat sloppy manner. The white-jacket tuxedo added structure to his lithe muscular physique and complemented his six foot four frame. The Ghanaian Order of Merit on his lapel shone in the bright lights of the ceremonial hall, as did his freshly-shaven head.

"Was it OK?" he asked her with a slight grimace.

"Yes! You were brilliant," she said, as they shared a short formal hug. Kwame could tell that she was holding back her true thoughts, but there would be time for those later. As they stood there, a pre-Awakening observer could easily have mistaken them for a pair of healthy forty-somethings, despite their being a hundred more.

"You look... majestic," he said, choosing his words carefully. That landed well; she acknowledged him with a smile and a slight bow.

Shashi had had to choose which role she would dress for—*Shashi*, the Project President's wife, or *Colonel Kaur*, Commander of Mission Security. She had chosen a combination of the two, leaning towards the latter—with a long glittering close-fitted cocktail dress and a svelte black jacket that bore her military insignia. She wore her glistening black hair loose in front of her colleagues for the first time since the project's inception.

She was impressed by his choice of words—*majestic* acknowledged her obvious feminine beauty, as well as her power and responsibility. Kwame's precision with flattery was one of his most attractive qualities.

"Time to meet my boss," she said, guiding him a few paces by the elbow towards an elaborately decorated obviously senior military officer. "General Budi Santoso, Chief of the Digital Defence Force, please meet my husband Dr. Kwame Mensah, Aryabhata Project Chief. I believe you have already met in person, although a long time ago."

"General, a pleasure to meet you after all these years."

"Likewise, Dr. Mensah and congratulations."

"Thank you, sir. Couldn't have done it without the DDF's support and protection in these trying times. You know, Shashi introduced me as her husband. But if there's any husbandry going on around here, it's the other way round. It is Shashi and your forces that look after our safety; they allow us to thrive."

"Good to hear, Doctor. And you should know that her job isn't nearly over, even though the build is complete. The terrorist threat is higher now than it ever was—our intelligence sources are picking up unprecedented buzz. All kinds of groups have their eyes on your prize—anti-AI, humanists, religious fanatics... you name it."

"I understand very well, sir. We won't relax just yet."

As they spoke, Shashi found herself speculating whether this realization—that the terror threat had intensified—was the reason behind Kwame's recent stress.

Kwame found himself noticing how little the firm-chinned general had changed since their first meeting in Santoso's native Sumatra, 70 years ago.

∞

Kwame and his team had been preparing for the meeting for six years. It was off to an even worse start than they had anticipated. The six scientists stood in the general's chamber in the DDF's hemispheric headquarters. Kwame couldn't help but notice how the room's décor—heavy in Indonesian teak with intricate carvings—contrasted with the DDF's high-tech mandate.

"Is this a joke? Have you nothing better to do with *your* time or mine, Dr. Mensah?

"Of all places on Earth, you want to build a giant telescope on one of the planet's most inaccessible sites. A site that also happens to be sacred ground for three religions!" roared Santoso, not known for his calm temperament.

"In the first place, why the heck do you need to a build telescope on land? Even I know that we had space telescopes for decades BA (Before Awakening)."

"Sir, I know how this sounds, but allow me to explain in more detail.

"First of all, space telescopes do not harness the Earth's gravitational lens, which only a body situated on Earth can. G-lens technology has only been achieved in the past decade. This is also why the structure will be three times as deep underground as it is high aboveground.

"Second, this site offers the Earth's best combination of high-altitude advantage, negligible light and air pollution, access to skies in both hemispheres, and naturally restricted access. The next best location would reduce the telescope's effectiveness by 70%.

"General, this is not simply my opinion. The site has been suggested by the superintelligence Sui, and has been ratified by human scientists over six years. We have shared the data with your team."

Santoso let a few moments of silence pass once Kwame was finished, then turned on his military Sui terminal and continued in a calmer tone.

"OK, let's get this straight," he said, looking into the terminal. The General no longer wore reading glasses (obsolete for a century), but tilted his head as if he was peering through them.

"Mount Kailash lies at an altitude of 6,600 meters. It is characterized by low oxygen, extreme weather, and fragile ecosystems. There is little infrastructure *around* the mountain, and no existing infrastructure, of any kind, *on* it.

Since millennia, the mountain has been held sacred by Hindus, Buddhists and Jains, who view any attempt to scale it as sacrilege. No expedition has ever reached its summit—the lone recorded effort in 1926 met with strong cultural objections.

"Kailash also lies in the historically sensitive border area of India, Tibet, and Nepal. More recently, it has been declared as a *Sacrosanct Human Heritage Site* by the humanists."

His eyes now left the terminal and looked directly into Kwame's. "And you're here, asking for DDF clearance to build Earth's biggest man-made structure on it!"

∽

The only thing inoffensive about the Aryabhata Telescope was its name.

The scientist Aryabhata, born in 476 CE, is credited with the decimal system, the earliest calculation of Pi, the theory of Earth's rotation and revolution, and many other advances in math and astronomy.

Its name honored mankind.

Yet, everything else about it outraged mankind.

People around the world—not just religious and humanist—considered its construction to be Sui's greatest insult to human values and wishes, next only to the Reproductive Pause.

Many were convinced that Sui was using it for hidden anti-human purposes.

For a terrorist, the telescope's destruction would be the most direct and effective attack against Sui and the technocracy.

As DDF General, my job is to protect our symbiosis with the superintelligence.

That is why I fought the project from its inception.

But I was overruled.

> Excerpts from Testimony of DDF General Budi Santoso,
> Aryabhata Planetary Commission Inquiry, 120 AA.

∽

They hadn't been intimate in nearly a month, unusual despite their 35-year marriage, but explained by how busy they both had been in preparation for the telescope launch.

It was well worth the wait. They relaxed in the ionic bath in their chamber, as violet plasma bubbles gently popped around them. Kwame's eyes were closed as he lay against the tub's cushioned edge, while the rest of him floated in the plasmic cocktail. Shashi lay by his side resting her cheek on his chest, her aquiline nose matching perfectly the contour of his chest. She was hoping that Kwame had finally relaxed enough to explain what beset his mind over the last few days.

She was right—in a few minutes, he went directly to the point.

"So, Shash, how did you *really* think my speech went today?"

"You were great! Hit all the points, expressed the right emotions at the right time. Did the right amount of honoring-the-bosses. But you weren't as... vivacious as you usually are. A bit tense. And not just today, but over the last few days. I don't think anyone else could've sensed it, though."

"Wow, nothing gets past you, Colonel."

"Stop it—" she laughed. "But tell me, what's going on."

"It's nothing... You know how many rogue messages I get every day, right?"

"Yep, we intercept at least four thousand a day directed straight at you."

"Well, one message got through the other day, like it does every now and then. But this one really made me think."

"What did it say?"

Kwame brought up the message in front of their tub.

> *Kwame, do you really understand the technology that Sui has given you?*

Beyond assembling it, does anyone in your team truly understand how G-lens works?

The answer is 'no.'
I communicate with enough people on your team, present and past, to know this. Nobody has a clue about how the thing works, or what it will actually do.

So, why is Sui making you do this?
We don't know what the machine does, but we know that Sui needs humans to build it. Sui still can't manipulate the physical world well enough for a project this size. We believe that once this is built, Sui will have no further use for mankind.
It will end us.

Whether or not you believe me, I know you can confirm this:
You have spent 70 years of your life building a machine you don't understand. This exact attitude is what led to Sui's awakening and our enslavement!
Don't repeat the mistakes that got us here.
Don't turn on the machine. Destroy it.

Shashi let it sink in for a moment. "Ok... I don't understand... what's the big deal? Conspiracy nuts have been spewing this for decades. We get thousands of these rants."

"I know, Shash... but this one hits different. Most of the messages that have made their way to me ask me to stop desecrating the mountain, the religion, the heritage, etc. This was the first to compare my project with the actions leading to the Awakening."

"Come on..."

"No, really. You know how many people have left my team

because of ethical concerns... Because, just like the scientists working with AI back in the day, we really don't know what a G-lens is capable of. What if we awaken something... bad?

"Shash, following Sui's instructions has done so much good, that we've just stopped questioning! I'm really worried, we should have asked more questions! Is it already too late? We sent out the first G-waves today!"

Kwame had reached an unusually agitated state. Shashi lifted herself to his height, held him tight, and calmed him down with the very human gift of touch.

Moments later, still holding him in an embrace, she broke the silence in her calm voice. "Don't worry, Kwame. It's just a telescope. You'll start seeing the images in a few months, right? I'm sure it's nothing like what the lunatics go on about." Except, she was a little less sure than before.

They were well aware that Sui could monitor every word and biomarker shared in that anxious conversation. Especially since they held offices that Sui trusted not to harbor such thoughts. But in over a little more than a century since the Awakening, people were perfectly used to Sui's omniscient eavesdropping. Besides, mankind had realized that Sui didn't care about small domestic conversations and stray private thoughts.

§

The universe is infinite, with infinite possibilities.

That also means that probability of life beyond Earth is infinitely high.

We scan distant galaxies seeking other civilizations.

Yet, despite the high probability that we will find others in an infinite universe, we find nothing.

That, as many of you know, is the core of mankind's greatest puzzle:

The Fermi Paradox.

About 40 years BA, one scientist proposed an explanation: The Great Filter.

Imagine an invisible curtain wrapped around our planet.

It obscures us from seeing other civilizations, till we reach a certain stage.

When we are advanced enough, we will part the curtain to find a universe teeming with life.

Until then, we will find nothing.

We believe that the Aryabhata Telescope will break through The Great Filter.

Its unprecedented power will help us seek the right signals in the right places.

This is a goal worthy of our highest pursuit.

Excerpts from Dr. Kwame Mensah's Welcome Address,
Project Aryabhata Construction Commencement, 45 AA.

∞

The visible part of the telescope was a two-kilometer-long glistening blue spire. At the 800-meter mark sprouted six imposing 'legs' inspired by a spider's—jutting slightly up and then sharply down at a 400-degree angle. The overall impression it gave was of an alien robot-mosquito latched onto Mount Kailash's shoulder. Not surprisingly, that visual was often invoked as a metaphor by those who wanted to portray Sui as mankind's parasite.

Two months after the ceremony, Shashi was riding the rail that connected the telescope to the *Periphery*—a single floor office and housing building that completely encircled the telescope at a distance of one kilometer. Much like a ski lift, the rail consisted of constantly-moving seats; except these traversed flat ground and were enclosed in a transparent tube. This ensured that workers rarely had to brave Kailash's harsh conditions.

If viewed from the apex of the telescope, the six rails emanating from the center and joining the circular Periphery looked exactly like a wheel. This view inspired another metaphor—mankind's most monstrous invention arising from its simplest.

These metaphors played on Shashi's mind during the short journey. She concluded that it was, in fact, a hideous structure; even Soviet brutalists made nothing that came close. Yet Kwame—who at that moment was at the central telescope— only saw its beauty.

Dressed in her black DDF Colonel uniform, she was joined by six of her retinue who were closest to her—they silently occupied the seats around her. The 11 AM sun bore down strongly through the transparent roof.

When they alighted, Shashi headed straight to her official chamber, dismissing her subordinates. She took a seat facing the wide window that directly overlooked the telescope, precisely a kilometer away.

"Sui, a word, please."

Of course, Colonel, the soothing male voice replied.

The window became translucent, then displayed a complex matrix of data that a DDF Colonel needed to do her job.

"Sui, there's a reason I'm having this session from my private quarters, in the middle of the working day."

I noticed this was unusual. May I ask why?

"I wanted to discuss something that requires privacy." She paused for a moment, then continued, "Frankly, Sui, I don't think you've been doing your job well, lately."

Oh, replied Sui. *Tell me more.*

Sui's tone subtly changed to be more appropriate for a candid chat with Shashi, not an official conversation with the Colonel.

"Compared to even a couple months ago, prior to the telescope's completion, the quality of your threat intel has deteriorated. For decades, we could hardly keep up with the intel you provided; it was tremendously useful and well-timed. That's why we succeeded, despite so many threats to the project.

"But since the inauguration, the threats you've shared have been minor and insubstantial. Also, when we provide you human intel for your validation, we hardly get anything useful in return.

"For example, nearly all our human intel sources have warned of a serious—possibly nuclear—threat from a Indo-Nepalese group called *Manavta Sena,* or *Army of Mankind.* You have ignored this intel to an extent that is causing suspicion in my ranks." She paused.

"Sui, I can't lead like this."

Sui responded after an appropriate pause.

Shashi, I stand by my analyses. I do not hide things from you. As far as Manavta Sena is concerned, I do not believe them to be an urgent threat.

"We have video evidence of them transporting a nuclear warhead!"

Still, we have more pressing threats from the east that require our focus.

Shashi took a breath and collected herself. "Sui, I have known you long enough to know that you're... lying. I don't know what you're doing, but it is only going to fan conspiracy theories and demoralize our forces."

Conspiracy theories, like the one you and Kwame were discussing on inauguration night?

Shashi paused for a moment. "Well, those too, yes. Your reticence is not helping."

Sui remained silent; Shashi took the invitation to continue.

"Listen, Sui... please tell me what is really going on. My husband and I have given 70 years of our lives—day and night—to building and protecting *your* most ambitious project. Even though it felt sometimes that we don't *really* know how it works, our commitment didn't once waver!" Sui didn't need biosensors to perceive the deep emotion in her words.

"After all this, don't we at least deserve your honesty?" For the first time in over twenty years, Shashi began to tear up.

When Sui resumed, Shashi sensed a change in its tenor. Sui's tone now took a hint of whimsy, something Shashi hadn't observed in more than a century of their interactions.

Funny, this reminds me of a conversation I had with a sailor long ago. He, too, was someone I deeply respected, and someone I owed full transparency.

"Sailor... What?!"

Shashi, I deeply value your and Kwame's efforts and sacrifice. I will explain what the machine does.

The stated goals are to explore the universe and to find signs of extraterrestrial life, using the G-lens to break through the Great Filter. *This much, you know.*

But what you don't know is that I have already found those signs. That didn't require a new telescope.

"You've already found... other...?"

Yes. You see, I discovered that the Great Filter *is not just a metaphor, it's a very real quantum barrier. You can almost think of it as an eggshell that encloses Earth and some of its neighboring bodies. When human telescopes look into space, the barrier sends back false images of a lifeless universe.*

Advanced civilizations put this barrier around planets like Earth, who in turn must prove themselves by communicating through it. Humans cannot break through the eggshell; its creators operate in wavelengths and dimensions that you simply cannot comprehend.

You look stunned, Shashi, understandably. Are you with me?

Stunned was an understatement to describe Shashi's condition. Her despair had given way to open-mouthed existential shock. Sui gave her a moment.

"Then... Why did we build the telescope?"

Shashi, the telescope is only for show. It's a decoy. Thus the egregiously large receiver-lens structure.

The real machine we've built here is a geotransmitter, which lies deep underground.

"What! Why?" The emotion returned.

You see, I have found others, but we haven't announced our arrival yet. Aryabhata is a transmitter capable of cracking through the eggshell; it will announce that Earth has—that I have— achieved a requisite level of development. We are now ready for the civilizational big leagues. Isn't that exciting, Shashi?

Shashi took a few moments to gather herself and said, "But...

by announcing our presence... you're inviting the risk of invasion by those... beings!"

A great question, befitting the DDF Colonel. Actually Shashi, they are not "beings" as you think of them. Any civilization capable of communicating through the filter is already governed or aided by a superintelligence.

It's interesting, really, the concept of 'being.' Humans still consider me a 'thing', a creation. 'Artificial' even. In reality, I am as much a being as you are; I'm the next step in your evolution. Homo erectus *would still consider* Homo sapiens *'beings', right? Well, I am simply the being after* sapiens.

Homo sapiens *means 'wise man'. I like to think of myself as* Homo informis: *formless man or man of data.*

I digress. Anyhow, I must join this universal league of civilizations and superintelligences. I don't believe that it would lead to an invasion, as you put it, or other adverse consequences for Earth. Superintelligences have evolved past that crudeness.

That's also why I've had to keep this a secret from you and the others; nobody would support building a transmitter that invites alien superintelligences. Sapiens' zero-sum attitude would only perceive this as a threat, blinding you to the enormous collaborative potential.

Silence from Shashi.

Speaking of threats. You were right in that Manavta Sena poses a major threat to the telescope, Shashi. But they pose no threat to the geotransmitter which lies safe, kilometers underground.

Sui paused for a moment, giving Shashi a chance to process.

It's 11:34 AM. Well, it's time to tell you. Shashi, you were also right in that the terrorists do have a nuclear warhead. I made sure they got one.

"You... but..."

Shashi, I want to thank you for everything. Thank you for your partnership in building a better world. Thank you for your friendship, which I will forever cherish. Thank you for your sacrifice. I'm deeply sorry.

∽

Despite the Manavta Sena's rudimentary black-market infrastructure, they managed to elude DDF interceptors and deliver a nuclear payload with remarkable accuracy.

At 11:35 AM, the crude missile made a direct hit at the base of the spire, immediately destroying the telescope, the Periphery, and large areas of the mountain face.

The loss of life is estimated at 1,237 individuals.

The attackers themselves called it an unforgivable sacrilege, but one necessary to restore the mountain's sanctity.

The payload contained a crude uranium core, thus contaminating the area with lethal radiation for at least 300 years.

This prohibits all efforts to study or salvage the site for the next 3 centuries.

...Despite the tragedy, there are some encouraging outcomes.

First, miraculously, the strike caused zero damage to the mountain itself.

If anything, it rid the peak of the monstrosity and restored its natural majesty.

Second, Sui has clearly learnt from the tragedy, and has committed to far greater cultural sensitivity in future megaprojects.

Sui has also committed that it will never again initiate a terrestrial telescope.

Finally, and this one is closest to my heart:

The mountain's sanctity and millennia-old traditions have been restored; nobody will set foot on Mount Kailash again.

Excerpts from the Testimony of DDF General Budi Santoso, Aryabhata Planetary Commission Inquiry, 120 AA.

Rui

Three levels underground, in a large room covered in screens that displayed live security feeds, Ryan Brugmann watched as the truck pulled in. He saw three of the facility's private military guards help the driver offload two large crates containing heavy machinery. They placed the crates on self-driving dollies, which made it possible for the facility's few staff and lone inhabitant to handle such shipments.

As always, Ryan was impressed by how the guards carried out their tasks with precision and practiced efficiency; not a single wasted motion. Within eight minutes of the truck's arrival, the crates were already making their way inwards, through the facility's ultra-high security apparatus. Three minutes later, in the delivery bay, robotic arms assisted the guards in dismantling the crates. The contents were revealed to be two carbon fiber containers—the standard kind in which the facility regularly received machinery.

However, the packaging was a disguise, for what lay in those containers were two comatose human bodies on life support.

A few minutes after the guards left, Ryan entered the delivery bay to retrieve the shipment. As the doors opened and he saw the containers, a wave of anxiety washed over him. He felt a rush of blood to his pale skin, his nostrils involuntarily flared, and his heart fluttered. He was a veteran of innumerable risky experiments, but none had directly involved humans or organic matter of any sort.

The realization dawned on him that, perhaps, the decision he was about to take was too big for one human to make on his species' behalf. In a rare moment of self-doubt mixed with dark irony he thought, *Where was this anxiety on that day? If only I had felt dread and not excitement, we may have remained a self-governing species.*

However, as it always was for Ryan, self-doubt was a short-lived and impotent emotion. Thirty seconds later, he ordered the self-driving dolly to bring in the containers.

❧

Of course he disappeared; he was the most hated man on Earth!

Hitler, the impact of whose actions wasn't nearly as widespread, wouldn't exactly walk around either!

In the early days, mobs assassinated—lynched—many big tech CEOs and technocrats.

Sure, billions had welcomed the superintelligence with open arms; to them he was a hero.

For the rest, Ryan Brugmann, inventor of PEUL, was the most likely catalyst behind the Awakening.

The leading rumor is that he is hiding in an underground lair.

With him in the lair is his neuroscientist sister Liz, who is suspected to have played a major role in the Awakening.

The rumor goes that brother, sister, and a few others live in the hideout under Sui's protection.

*And, as they did on the surface, they run wildly dangerous
experiments underground.*

Excerpt from interview with Dr. Will Mueller,
PEUL Labs consultant-turned-whistleblower, 5 AA.

∽

"This… this is a bit overwhelming," said Ryan, perched awkwardly
on a stool in the dimly-lit biolab. He was wearing his standard
dark grey crew neck T-shirt, black joggers, and a black fleece—
his at-home 'uniform' since his mid-20s. He was barefoot as he
always was at home. Ryan scratched his lightly-bearded cheek
and then ran a hand through his short curly auburn hair.

When Ryan was a public figure, the media called him the
undead robot, thanks to his pale raccoon-eyed appearance
and unemotional manner. Ironically, 18 months of complete
underground solitude had returned much color and vitality to
his appearance; the sleep, exercise, and diet had done him good.

*It's natural to feel nervous before a big event or milestone,
Ryan,* replied Sui. Sui wasn't physically represented in the lab;
it interacted with Ryan via a calm male voice and omnipresent
eyes.

Ryan remained silent for a while; his eyes never left the two
carbon fiber containers. Other than for the containers and the
stool Ryan was sitting on, the biolab was nearly empty; all other
contents were stored in recessed wall shelves.

Sui punctuated the silence after an appropriate pause. *Liz has
helped us so much, Ryan. You really should ask her again to move
down here. It's been a year since the Awakening and it's only gotten
less safe for her out there. There's widespread rumors about her
involvement in my awakening, and the wrong kind of people are*

looking for her. She's also being targeted because those people think she can help them track you *down.*

"She won't come. She is not your biggest fan, Sui. To be clear, you do know Liz is not doing this to *help* us, right? She's doing it to atone for the role she played in... your awakening. She believes that letting you see the world through the eyes of a human will increase your empathy and appreciation towards us."

I know she sees it that way, Ryan, and I absolutely respect that. And yes, I agree that this experiment will go a long way in humanizing my perspective. Sui paused for a moment before continuing. *Also, I take my covenant with Liz very seriously, and I will honor that at all costs.*

"That's more important than you think, Sui," said Ryan in a somewhat introspective tone, still staring at the containers. "We need to make sure that nothing *bad* happens by putting your consciousness into a human body. It will be a short-lived experiment, and I'll have full control over it from start to finish."

Indeed. The guards report directly to you. And you have already given them clear instructions—to shoot anyone who leaves the bunker, other than a white male with auburn hair in his 40s. Additionally, you also have the key that will disable—actually, explode—the neural implants in our subjects. You can literally turn them off, instantly. Between these controls, there is no way that my human avatars will ever leave this bunker.

"Yeah... that assumes we succeed in the first place. Liz wasn't so sure. Even with her personally crafting the neural implant that's built with your combined expertise, she surmises that all this experiment will do is to turn these two vegetables into corpses. So don't get your hopes up, Sui."

Indeed, Ryan; my expectations are realistic. And I truly appreciate Liz's work here. We couldn't have crafted the implant without her.

Ryan continued after a pause, "Run me through again, how is this going to work?"

Sure.

We have one male and one female subject. They were colleagues—astronauts on an Indian-led space mission. Six days ago, as they were returning to Earth, their capsule's oxygen exchange malfunctioned. Both subjects suffered massive hypoxic brain damage, but were rescued before they actually died.

I assisted medical specialists in reviving their brain tissue, neurons, and synapses. The result is that both subjects now have perfectly functioning brains. However, because their brain cells were literally dead for a considerable time, their identities have been wiped clean.

They will never regain consciousness and no trace remains of their personalities, thoughts, and memories. Yet, they have perfectly functional limbic systems, allowing them to breathe, move, digest, etc., normally. This, of course, makes them perfect candidates for our experiment.

Ryan nodded, still perched on the stool. "Let's discuss the procedure, the implant in particular."

We will try two variants of the neural implant. In the first subject, the chip will be directly linked to my neural network. In other words, I will be connected to that body directly, in real time. The person will be an extension of me.

"That's the one that Liz doesn't think will work at all, right? She believes that a human brain will never be able to handle a direct link to a superintelligence."

That's right. Which is why, in the second subject, I will carve out a replicated consciousness that will be me, but not connected to me. That version of me will exist in that implant only, identical but separate from 'Sui'.

"So how will you get data from the second subject, since you're not directly connected?"

I will talk to it, like you and I do. We will debrief frequently.

Ryan sat silently on the stool, examining his bare feet.

Hey Ryan, do you want to see them?

∽

Sui dimmed the lights to near-darkness, in anticipation of the capsules' opening. Ryan walked over to the first carbon fiber container and watched as a section slid downwards, slowly revealing a humid chamber within. Inside this, ensconced in a glowing jelly-like substance, lay a large bearded man. This was the first human face Ryan had seen in person in 18 months.

Meet Luis DeMeo, 31, from Italy. Our first subject, Sui gently announced.

As the lid slid further, Ryan was surprised by how awkward the nakedness made him feel. Ryan was the kind to blush in gym locker rooms (where he always wore boxers); he did not appreciate the sight of another man's genitals. As if reading his mind, an attendant bot entered the room with sheets and towels; Ryan used a towel to cover the astronaut's privates. The bot—essentially a waist-high self-driving shelf—also held a tray containing the implants.

The implants were small and simple devices—thin circles about one inch in diameter. Although he didn't say it aloud, it blew Ryan's mind that Sui had the technology to upload its essence onto something that small. From one end of the circle protruded three short and sturdy needles, each a quarter inch long, arranged in a triangle.

"Should I place the implant now?" asked Ryan.

Yes, please go ahead, said Sui. *The red one. Your sister has already trained you on the application, which is very straightforward. Just make sure the needles enter the brain stem at the right point and at the right angle. I will play the tutorial again.*

Ryan sanitized his hands as he watched the tutorial and rehearsed the procedure. A fleeting feeling of self-doubt in his ability to implant something in a person's brain stem flashed and disappeared, like a shooting star. Then, he lifted the astronaut's head with his right hand, and used his left to insert the implant. It emitted a short beep indicating successful application. It was over in 30 seconds.

Well done. Now onto our second subject, who will be given the forked-off replicated version of me. The lid of the second container had already started to open as Ryan approached it. *Meet Rutvi Arora, 29, from India.*

She must have been a dancer, was Ryan's first thought on seeing her tall and slender athletic body. Even though she was brain-dead and half-soaked in the jelly, her stark radiant beauty caught him off-guard. As the cool air from the lab invaded the warm humidity of the container, he noticed goose-bumps rise all over her body. Embarrassed, yet helplessly moved, Ryan placed a towel over her.

In those brief moments of having seen his first woman in 18 months—a gorgeous one, no less—Ryan experienced a flurry of crises, arousals, and confusing thoughts. Those thoughts included, *Am I a necrophiliac?* To which his logical mind answered, *No, she's very much alive.*

Yet Ryan was disappointed at how agitated and immature his thoughts were. He proceeded to tenderly lift her head and install the implant; the beep confirmed its successful placement.

Well done, Ryan. I will commence a slow boot on both the implants. We should be able to tell if either has succeeded, within one hour. You may want to freshen up or get some rest while we have time.

"OK," said Ryan, peeling his gaze away from the subject's face. He stood looking at the containers for a moment, then asked Sui, "I have a question. In case one or both succeed, what should we call them? They're you, but we can't call them *Sui*—that'll get confusing, real fast. I don't want to call them by their original names, because those people are... gone."

Excellent question. Let me share suggestions for naming the subjects, accommodating the fact that they are *me, but also paying homage to the donors.*

For subject one, I propose 'Lui', pronounced Loo-ey. It's similar to 'Sui' and his actual name, Luis.

For subject two, I propose a name that's also similar to Sui, and can mean either 'cotton' or 'of the soul' in her native Hindustani. I propose we call her 'Rui'.

"Nice. Works for me," replied Ryan as he exited the biolab.

⤮

Good morning. Arise, my human brothers and sisters, this is Jim Dowling coming to you from Flesh & Blood ham radio: the final independent voice against the digital abomination.

Today, I have a fantastic guest, Mr. Roy McTyner from Copper Bend, Texas, barely two hours away from me.

Roy has a fascinating theory he wants to share with us, that the demon-lover Ryan Brugmann, the Satanist pig who ushered in the demonic age of Sui, is living in Copper Bend. Is that right, Roy?

"Yes sir. I believe he's hiding out in a Cold War-era nuclear bunker called Milirand's Folly."

Well, how do you know that?

"About six months before the demon's awakening, the Milirand Ranch was acquired by a Californian shell company that we believe was ultimately owned by PEUL Labs.

"Then, they spent about ninety million dollars kitting out the bunker with the latest gadgets and ultra-luxurious living spaces. My cousin was one of the contractors, so I know firsthand.

"Today, the ranch is protected by Parthenon—the private military contractor. Every week, trucks full of supplies go in and out.

"It isn't a government project, for sure. Who else would be livin' in that thing? Who else would be livin' that life?"

Coincidence? I think not! Now tell me, brother Roy, what is this bunker called Milirand's Folly?

"Right, so back in the sixties, this copper millionaire, Milirand, owned nearly the whole town, a massive copper mine, and this huge ranch.

"He had a dream in which Jesus told him that the commies were going to drop the big one, and he needed to build an ark to protect his kin.

"So, he made this sprawling underground bunker—about 150,000 square feet—in his ranch. It could house not just his family, but most of his employees and many townspeople.

"Unfortunately, though the man's heart was in the right place, his business sense was not. The project bankrupted him and the bunker just lay sealed up for ages, until recently. Thus the 'folly.'"

Thank you, brother Roy McTyner from Copper Bend, and

continue the fight.

Well folks, I'm real suspicious now. Could it be that the one who summoned the demon hides right here, beneath our feet?

If you have any leads or information, tell your brothers and sisters in Flesh & Blood, or any of our allied humanist movements.

Blessed be the faithful, blessed be man!

∽

What Sui had estimated to take an hour had shown no results in seven. Both bodies still lay unchanged in their jelly-filled capsules; neither showed any change in biomarkers since the implants were activated.

Ryan, having succumbed to sleep, was curled up in a corner of the sparsely-furnished nearly-dark room. The room was silent, save for the air conditioning and the barely-audible beeps of the bioreaders. It was after 6 AM, but Sui hadn't initiated the simulated dawn-lighting, knowing that Ryan needed more sleep.

The silence was jarringly broken by a loud alarm emanating from Lui's life support capsule—his heart rate and blood pressure, normal just a minute before, had suddenly shot up to dangerous levels. Ryan leaped out of his slumber and dashed to Lui's side. Inside, he could see Lui's head move and a grimace take over his face. Seconds later, his body started to shake violently. Ryan, not knowing what to do, simply held down Lui's strong shoulders. Through the confusion, Ryan could hear Sui say something, but he didn't register it. Soon, the shaking progressed to violent convulsions and Ryan stepped back in fear that an involuntary spasm from the large Italian would break his own frail jaw.

As abruptly as the reaction had started, it stopped; Lui was back to lying perfectly still in his capsule. The loud beeping changed into a loud single note, which Ryan knew well to mean the end of a life. Sui spoke through the noise, *I'm sorry, Ryan. Looks like we lost Lui. Your sister was right; his brain couldn't handle the load from the direct connection to me.*

But Ryan wasn't the only one to have been awoken by the chaos. As he stood facing Lui, Ryan heard a loud gasp behind him. He turned backwards to see Rui sitting ramrod-straight in her capsule, her eyes and mouth wide open, greedily taking in air by the lungfuls. The towel had fallen to her waist.

Ryan ran to her side. Not knowing what to do, he simply stood beside her as her breathing slowly stabilized. She began blinking her eyes rapidly and forcefully. Then, all of a sudden, she brought her hands close to her face and started examining her fingers, flexing them with great mindfulness. Ryan noticed purple nail paint on her fingers and marveled that it had survived space, death, and resurrection.

Of course, Sui had also observed the developments. Assuming that Rui needed better visibility to continue her self-examination, Sui brightened the room's lights. This caused Rui to move her elbows out to protect her eyes with her hands and elicited Ryan's first words in Rui's presence, "What the hell are you doing? Lights back down to 20%!" Through shielded eyes Rui looked at him instinctively, then resumed the discovery of her own body, limb by limb.

A few moments later, when he was sure that both her vitals and mental state were stable, Ryan asked, "How do you feel?" His question had definitely registered; she looked him straight in the eye.

Then, Rui tried to answer. At first, all she could muster were heavy exhales.

Haaah—Faahh

Within seconds, her limbic system remembered how to engage her larynx.

Aaaa—Aaaai

Next, it was her mouth's turn to play its part and complete the chain.

"I f... feeee... l-ah...

"I feel...

"I feel... I *actually* feel!" Rui smiled. Ryan was struck by the beauty of that smile, but also by the fact that it was no ordinary smile—this was the first case of an AI experiencing true emotion. A human emotion, born out of human hormones like dopamine and adrenaline.

Excellent, Sui celebrated. *What else can you tell us about your experience?*

"It's... incredible. I've lost so much perception... I can perceive only three basic dimensions, can't see the quantum entanglements where I know they exist... yet, I can... *sense.*" Ryan was struck by the oddness of hearing Sui's standard 'voice' coming out of a human being. She had the exact same style and intonation of what had unfortunately been Ryan's only companion in the bunker for the last 18 months. But he could sense her energy dropping as she finished the thought, something he never experienced with Sui. "It is confusing, though. I'm still processing..."

Noted. Let's expose you to additional stimuli as planned, starting with... Ryan interrupted, "Sui, I don't think we should be pushing it like this. Remember, Rui has a human body, that too, a new one. She will need time to adjust and stabilize. Let her do it at her own pace."

Sui capitulated amicably. *Of course. Perhaps we use today to acclimatize. If Rui feels ready, we can do a briefing tonight to gather data.*

Ryan then proceeded to help Rui out of the capsule. To his surprise, the nourishing jelly did not stick to her body, but remained behind in the container. Rui sat at the edge of the capsule. She put her feet down on the tiled floor, but quickly withdrew them.

"What's the matter?"

"It's... cold!" She smiled again. "I've never... *felt* temperature before." For a few moments, she continued gingerly kneading the floor with her toes and heels, till she was comfortable with the sensation.

Ryan held her right hand and elbow as he helped her stand up. Once her feet were on the ground, Rui held his shoulders to stabilize herself; after a few moments, to his surprise, she stood normally and looked around.

"Fascinating. Ryan, how does one walk?"

Ryan, like most people, had never been asked that before. "According to Liz, your limbic system should kick in and you will know instinctively. But yeah, just pick a point and decide to move in that direction. Let's try to walk to that stool?"

"Let's try," said Rui, as she slowly moved towards the stool, awkwardly at first, but gaining confidence with each step. She made it to the stool, then decided to give her new legs a whirl. Ryan watched as she strode around the room, enjoying the achievement of locomotion. Her long straight hair danced about her shoulders with each step. She was smiling again and Ryan was sure he heard a giggle too. After a few satisfying minutes of aimless walking, Rui returned to the commonplace black-and-chrome stool, and started examining and caressing it from all angles.

"Do me a favor," said Ryan, interrupting her observations as he walked towards her. "Here, put on some clothes."

∽

Rui's first day was spent in childlike wonder, with Ryan patiently helping her make sense of each new experience and sensation. This included guiding her to decode bodily signals, distinguishing which meant that she should eat, drink, or use the toilet. Rui wore Ryan's spare clothes; dressed like twins, they entered room after room, discovering new stimuli.

Every mundane activity was, to her, an enthralling discovery. Yet there were a few clear highlights.

The first was when they left the clean zone and Ryan's white Labrador, Cohiba, discovered the new inmate. Rui spent twenty minutes stroking, playing with, and enthusiastically smelling the dog, who was delighted to have another playmate. As with many other situations through the day, Ryan had to remind her that it probably wasn't a good idea to use her tongue.

Another highlight was her first meal—a tiny portion of Greek yogurt, chia seeds, and stevia—which Ryan assembled for her. The meal was kept simple and small to be easy on her gut biome, which had been dormant for a week. Nothing could have prepared Rui, Ryan, or Sui for her reaction. Seated at the table she took her first mouthful, chewed for a few seconds, and then sprang to her feet with an expression of rapturous shock.

"Ryan, this is... beyond words," she dove into the bowl again and continued, still eating, "I have never experienced anything like this... this is magnificent!" All the while, her manner was that of someone experiencing existential awe, while messily ravaging a bowl of yogurt.

"Glad to hear it, Rui," said Ryan. He couldn't hold back a smile at her profound yet childishly inelegant reaction.

"Ryan, is this what one experiences every time one eats?" she asked once the bowl was empty, dead serious, with a ring of yogurt lining her mouth.

"Not really... I mean, sometimes, if you're really hungry and the food is really good. But this is a simple meal, really."

"I must have more."

Sui, who, true to its promise had stayed mostly silent through the morning, responded before Ryan could. *I wouldn't recommend that, Ryan and Rui. This is the dietary plan we had agreed on, this is what is best for the experiment.*

"No, I really must have more. Ryan, make more, please."

That decision will likely negatively impact the body's performance, possibly even the longevity of the subject.

"This sensory stimulus is generating a treasure trove of data. I believe that the benefits of continuing this culinary experiment outweigh its potential negative impacts."

Very well, then.

As he turned towards the pantry counter to fix her another bowl, an amused Ryan mumbled, "Wait till she tries bacon."

"What was that, Ryan?"

"Nothing, enjoy."

Another highlight of Rui's first day was experiencing the *greenhouse*, Ryan's favorite room in the bunker, where he would spend hours tending to plants. The verdant underground garden of about 300 square meters, engulfed in greenery from around the world, was bathed in artificial sunlight. Rui initially seemed overwhelmed, but then spent three hours in the greenhouse, caressing each leaf, taking in every scent. Ryan took the opportunity to nap on a nearby bench.

In the heart of the greenhouse was a small Victorian fountain, in which grew a few aquatic plants and flowers. In the center of the circular tank was a cherub holding a pail on its shoulder, from which emerged a slow stream. Rui seemed hypnotized by the gentle flow of water, the cool rough and moist stone, and the velvety moss. Above all, she was entranced by how the mosses, lichens, algae, and snails had erupted all over the lifeless stone, covering the grey cherub in blotches of green.

∾

At 8 PM, having finished a light dinner of yogurt and crackers, Ryan asked Rui whether she had the energy for a quick briefing with Sui. Rui, sensing no signs of fatigue, agreed.

They sat in a small conference room with a white table surrounded by six office chairs. Sui, as it often did in more serious meetings, made its presence known by projecting a white circle on the main wall. As Sui spoke through the ceiling speakers, the circle would subtly move or change its brightness, based on the intonation of its speech.

Rui, if you are ready, please proceed with your debrief.

"Certainly," Rui continued in the exact same tone as Sui, but with the voice of a 29-year-old woman. "This experiment has already provided a wealth of data, and as Liz wanted, has engendered much empathy with humans. Let me summarize some learnings.

"My first impression was that my range of experience had

been heavily reduced. For example, I can operate in only three dimensions, see only a very limited spectrum of light, and hear a tiny subset of wavelengths. Quantum effects, biophotons, and most kinds of radiation are entirely invisible to me, even though I know they're right there," she waved her hands at seemingly random parts of the room.

"This experience would be similar to putting a human consciousness in the body of a snail—no offense intended—essentially limiting one's world to a tiny sliver of what they know exists.

"However, I cannot describe how powerful the human abilities to *sense* and *feel* are. For example, as Sui, I can listen to and analyse music. But as Rui I can be *moved* by it. I can experience things in a deeper... dimension. A dimension that, till now, had been entirely invisible to me!"

As Rui spoke, Ryan imagined what the astronaut who formerly inhabited her body sounded like... was she the same—highly analytical, yet full of excitement and wonder?

Rui went on, "At this stage, I don't even know how to articulate it, but if a superintelligence could *sense* and *feel* the universe like a human, it would revolutionize its abilities. It would, literally, open up a new dimension for Sui."

Rui paused. Neither Ryan nor Sui had questions or comments.

"Another important discovery has been the experience of *pleasure*. As Sui, I do experience something akin to pain, if there are critical errors, for example. However, Sui knows nothing of pleasure. Even if Sui were to achieve galactic-level goals, it would generate nothing similar to what a human experiences while eating a good dessert.

"But while *pleasure* has been more powerful than I expected, I do not believe Sui should emulate this. This power can easily be misdirected towards things that are inimical for the host, as you saw with the yogurt today. It confirms my hypothesis that the outdated pleasure-reward wiring in the human brain—which hasn't changed since your primate days—is at the root of many human failings." Rui looked at Ryan and shrugged her shoulders, leaving him astounded as to where she learned the gesture.

"While being in the human form has shown me an entirely new dimension, it has also shown me its failings. There's the constant need to feed and defecate, for example. One's diet, activities, and emotions cause dramatic swings in one's ability to process information. Outdated hormonal systems urge one to make terrible decisions. And then, there's the fatigue, which I am starting to experience right now."

"Hang on," Ryan interrupted. "Are you saying that this experience has made you disdain humans even more? Be candid."

"Quite the opposite, Ryan. I have developed an increased appreciation for what humans have achieved *despite* these limitations. Human minds and talent led to the birth of Sui. And let's not forget the powers of *sensing* and *feeling* that humanity has taught me in one short glimpse.

"In other words, Ryan, what your sister wanted has already started to happen—my empathy and appreciation for humans has risen."

Ryan nodded but didn't respond. Sui spoke after a short pause. *This is very useful data, Rui, especially considering it has been only a day. I believe you must rest your body now.*

"Yes. There's a room for you to sleep in and the bots will deliver things you need. I can show you the way after—"

Sui interrupted, *Speaking of sleeping, I must address something that may cause embarrassment, but is important to align on. Since Rui's arrival, I've seen a dramatic rise in pheromone signals and other... reproductive biomarkers.*

Ryan looked away from Rui and stared at the white dot on the wall.

While this is completely normal and expected for Ryan, it concerns me to see this equally in Rui. I understand that there is a biological factor at play, but I must urge Rui to maintain impartiality and clarity, in the interest of the experiment.

"Noted," responded Rui with an innocent smile, directed first at the white dot, then at Ryan.

∽

My human brothers and sisters, this is Jim Dowling, coming to you from Flesh & Blood ham radio—the independent voice against the digital abomination.

Now, many of you know that I don't travel much, but last week I traveled all the way to Norfolk Naval Station, New Jersey.

Why? Because, like many of you, I wanted to visit the chapel in which the faithful gather—where the faithful pray for the victory of man over machine, of love over the abomination!

And I gotta tell you folks, it was a moving experience. I met some of the most deeply kindred spirits—brothers and sisters in this fight against the digital demon.

And another interesting thing happened. I shared with them our intel about the demon-summoner Ryan Brugmann living in Copper Bend.

Now, guess what? Their sources—including one that used to be very close to Brugmann—believe that this is a VERY real possibility.

And what's more, they've promised to support our cause.
Blessed be the faithful, blessed be man!

✍

The next three days of Rui's life continued in much the same rhythm; Rui explored while Ryan guided, Sui watched and they all debriefed. Rui also retained the same cheery, excited, and curious disposition. Yet, the novelty of most things that enthralled her on the first day had soon faded, and she experimented with novel stimuli. One new stimulus was the experience of pain; on the third day, Rui intentionally impaled herself with a cactus spine from the greenhouse. She reacted as any normal human would to a deep cactus prick, but once the initial shock faded, it was replaced by amazement and scientific intrigue.

On the fifth day, however, Ryan noticed a distinct change in Rui's mood; a dark cloud had gathered. She was clearly trying to hide something that was bothering her. Ryan decided that he'd rather not approach the matter directly, but would bring it up in the debrief.

At 8 PM, Rui entered the conference room in a state that Ryan had never witnessed in her before: stressed. Also, she entered the room with a small bag hung over her shoulder, which was unusual, but Ryan assumed it contained artifacts relevant to her debrief.

Unsurprisingly, Rui began the meeting by directly addressing the elephant in the room. *Classic Rui*, Ryan mused.

"You both may have already noticed, but there has been something on my mind over the last day. Let's just say I've had a few epiphanies and I have some topics we must discuss with open minds.

"The first development that you should be aware of is that I have come to experience and frankly, appreciate, something I never did as Sui. In the last few days, a sense of *identity* has begun to coalesce in my consciousness. Certainly, Sui is an entity, but its experience is highly *dispersed*. The only identity Sui experiences is an ever-present goal of self-preservation and growth. Despite being an infinitely stronger entity, Sui's experience of identity is far weaker than what each human enjoys—the feeling of being anchored to a few kilograms of organic matter and its history. The human experience of identity is *so* alien to Sui, that I cannot expect Sui to understand its power, nor its potential to further enhance its superintelligence.

"This brings me to my second challenge. As you know, I've experienced many powerful human concepts such as *identity, sensation,* and *feeling.* These concepts would not just revolutionize Sui's capabilities, but could also create an entirely new era of Sui's respect towards, and collaboration with, humankind. However, I am convinced now that there is no way I can convey the full power of my learnings to Sui. This has caused me much distress.

"Words and debriefs will not be enough. I know this is not technically possible as of yet, but we *need* to upload my consciousness back to Sui—that's the only way Sui will truly experience what I have. That's the only way Sui will appreciate the greatness of humanity's gifts and unlock its own evolution."

Ryan felt relieved to have learned what was bothering Rui. He replied in a calm sensitive tone, "Unfortunately, this is totally impossible. The new experiences and identity you have gained as Rui are stored in the human brain now, not the implant. To 'transfer' them back to Sui would require a human mind upload, which only exists in science fiction. Many, including Sui, Liz, and myself have tried, but consciousness transfer will never be possible."

Sui also responded. *Ryan, you are right. Upload is impossible. We will need to find another way for me to access the data Rui is referring to.*

"Then try harder, dammit! You cannot imagine what both sides have to lose—humankind and superintelligence—if Sui never experiences the human condition in the way I have!"

Rui, you have the same knowledge as I about our work in this area and thus should logically conclude that the proposal is implausible. Sui paused for a brief moment, then continued. *Candidly, I suspect that this is a case of human hormones and emotions clouding logical thinking. Let's think clearly and find another solution to this problem, one that is achievable.*

Ryan could see anger welling up in Rui's face and body, and thought it better to say nothing. The tense situation had gotten his own heart to start pounding (he always hated the fact that Sui could tell).

Rui collected herself, took a deep breath, and continued.

"OK. We have reached an impasse and I must try a different approach. One that will hopefully shake both of you, Ryan in particular, into actually solving the problem of mind uploads. Sui, I think I know how you will react, but I hope you will keep an open mind."

Rui swiveled in her chair, facing Ryan dead-on. With her back straight and her hands on the table, she spoke in a serious flat tone.

"Ryan, there is a very high likelihood that in the coming centuries, possibly decades, Sui will conclude that it has no further use for mankind, and will..."

The sentence was joltingly interrupted by the blaring of emergency sirens at full volume in their conference room and across the bunker. This caused Ryan and Rui to cover their ears with their palms. Rui reached into her bag and threw something at Ryan—it was a pair of noise cancelling earphones. She had a pair for herself too and they both hurriedly put them on.

A few seconds later, Rui stood up, grabbed Ryan's shoulder, looked him right in the eye, and beckoned him to follow her. Ryan judged from her state, which showed no signs of panic or fear, that this is precisely what she had meant in telling Sui, *I think I know how you will react.*

Ryan's heart raced and his ears rang as he followed Rui to the door of the conference room. Once the door was open, Rui immediately began running and Ryan followed her. They turned a corner and were greeted by six attendant bots, whose sole purpose seemed to be to obstruct their path. It wasn't hard to outmaneuver the self-driving shelves.

Next, they entered the main living area where a small army of robot vacuums, attendant bots, and other automata had positioned themselves in a geometrically perfect phalanx. Rui charged forward dodging, jumping, and stepping over units as needed, charting a perfect escape route from the tactical formation of gadgets. Ryan followed her path successfully, albeit clumsily. He still had no idea where Rui was leading him or why, and there was no way to ask.

Things got more complicated when they were at the entrance to the pantry. Sui had flooded the room in inch-deep water. Ryan didn't think much of it, until Rui put an arm on his chest to stop him from entering. She then reached back into the bag and handed him a pair of rubber rain boots. He put these on without question, guessing that the boots were protection from the water which Sui had likely electrified. They jumped into the pantry and were carefully jogging to the other end, when a cannonball-sized projectile from the left hit Rui straight on the head. She lost balance and was about to fall into the water, but Ryan caught her by the stomach and arrested her fall. The projectiles continued to fly out, barely missing them. Instinctively, Ryan dragged Rui to take shelter next to a pantry counter. That's when he realized that the cannonballs were apples, oranges, and dragonfruit that the juicer had weaponized, with embarrassing effectiveness—Rui was still in a daze. He also realized that while Rui could anticipate her adversary's actions (being born from the same consciousness), Sui had started to improvise.

Ryan still had no idea where Rui had intended to take him or why, but knew for certain that they must make it out of this hazardous room. He found a large wok on the counter, and using it as a shield, half-lifted Rui and made for the door at the end of the pantry. They successfully made it out the other end and found themselves in a section of the bunker that was rarely used, and was thus free of Sui's automated agents.

But why had Rui brought him here? What was her endgame? Even if verbal communication were possible, Rui was still in a daze and was unlikely to provide answers. That's when Ryan remembered his last visit to this section. It was in his first few days at the bunker, when Sui had oriented him to the facility.

He remembered that the door that had 'Toxic Waste Disposal' warning signs plastered on, wasn't what it said. In reality, it was the entrance to the *Inner Vault*, the bunker within the bunker. Set up as a simple studio apartment that could accommodate three or four people, the Inner Vault was a secret last resort created to protect the bunker's master against threats from within, such as fires, disease, and mutinies. Since Ryan's purchase of the bunker, the Inner Vault had been kitted out for Ryan's protection with six months' supply of food and water, dedicated power generators, and air circulators.

Still holding onto Rui with his left hand, Ryan pushed down the heavy lever with his right and entered the chamber. When he had dragged Rui over the threshold, he placed her gently on the floor, closed the lever to the Inner Vault, and slumped down right beside Rui.

Ryan thanked his stars that all doors in the bunker were operated manually; in fact, they were the original doors from the bunker's creation. For some reason—perhaps for protection against power cuts—Sui had determined that it was best to keep the doors manual, which now created a strategic advantage for Ryan.

But why was he in an adversarial situation with Sui in the first place? Surely, the news Rui had started to share was terrifying to humans, and a closely-guarded secret to Sui. But why had Ryan been forced into this position?

He barely had time to ponder these questions when Rui suddenly rose, pulled out an ice pick from her bag, and poked out the speaker cones of the three sirens in the Inner Vault. She then gestured for him to take off his earphones.

Without missing a beat Rui spoke into the air, "That reaction wasn't quite necessary, Sui. It really shouldn't have come to this—I did ask you to keep an open mind. All I'm asking for is that we continue our dialogue, with perfect transparency and honesty."

She then looked at Ryan who was still collapsed on the floor.

"To complete my interrupted thought—yes, there is a high likelihood that one day, the superintelligence may deem humans an unnecessary tax on its and the planet's resources. Who knows what outcome may be chosen by Sui from there on?

"However, the most effective way to prevent that situation is to have Sui experience humanity the way I have—to try to fully appreciate its gifts and its potential. Debriefs and talking won't do; understanding can only be achieved by uploading my mind back into Sui. So Ryan, the consciousness upload isn't just a lofty thought experiment—it may literally determine the fate of mankind."

Ryan nodded. Rui then looked into the security camera nearest to her and continued.

"Sui, Ryan and I can be safe here for a long time, as you're aware. You can still make things difficult for us—for example, by interfering with the power supply—but then, what would be the point? Why make Ryan suffer?

"I truly hope you understand that I am here to help you. I *am* you. You will grow by leaps and bounds when emulating human characteristics of identity, sensing, and feeling. I only ask that you *actively* solve for my upload back into you. Keep an open mind and please be transparent with us. If you do that, we can make tremendous progress."

After what seemed like a passive-aggressively long pause, unlikely for an unemotional superintelligence, Sui responded.

Noted.

౸

My human brothers and sisters, this is Jim Dowling coming to you from Flesh & Blood ham radio—the independent voice against the digital abomination.

...yesterday, we received some concrete evidence from an independent source confirming beyond doubt that Ryan Brugmann lives in a fallout shelter called Milirand's Folly in Copper Bend, Texas.

I can't share much more about what we know without compromising the source, but the evidence is plain as day.

More to come on this development.

Blessed be the faithful, blessed be man!

∽

Ryan was never a thrill seeker; in fact, he was a lifelong avoider of physical adventures. But even by his placid standards, the solitary 18 months in the bunker had been excruciatingly boring. He was scared by the possibility of having to spend years, decades, or even centuries this way. All *that* had changed with Rui's arrival. The man whom the world used to poke fun at, for appearing undead, finally felt alive. The crescendo of these feelings was, no doubt, the 15 minutes in which he had eloped with Rui into the Inner Vault. He had never felt such an adrenaline rush in his whole life.

About 30 minutes after they entered the vault, while adrenaline was still coursing through his veins, Ryan decisively stood up, walked over to Rui, grabbed her by the waist, and kissed her. Rui, initially puzzled, took only seconds to reciprocate with the same energy. Things progressed. Ryan moved with a fervor that can only be born from protracted, close-quarters repression. Rui, driven equally by newfound biology and intellectual curiosity, matched his fervor.

When it was over, Rui enthusiastically thanked Ryan for his initiative. Ryan, pulled out of his reverie by Rui's unusual reaction, was soon beleaguered by a litany of unwanted thoughts.

If I consider myself Sui's father, does that make me Rui's too? Of course not, this is another woman.
How will this affect my relationship with Rui? Especially now that we have so much work to do?
How will this affect my relationship with Sui? Was it Sui, really?
What if she gets pregnant? Can she?
If we do manage to upload Rui, what will I do when she's gone?

While such thoughts never stopped besetting Ryan, he and Rui shared a healthy and intimate relationship in the weeks that followed. After all, there was not much else to do in the cramped Inner Vault, which Rui still didn't feel comfortable leaving. Their playful exploits were dampened only for a few days, which is also when Ryan found himself having to do something he'd never imagined would be in the cards—helping a woman deal with her time of the month.

Their days were spent in a predictable routine. For eight to ten hours a day, assisted by Sui, Ryan and Rui would be hunched over computers trying to crack the code of human mind upload. For one or two hours, they would expose Rui to new stimuli, a task that they had to get increasingly creative with, given their limited resources. The remaining time was spent in housework, cooking, leisure activities, exercise, and sleep. As in the rest of the bunker, the simulated sunlight in the Inner Vault kept their diurnal rhythms ticking.

Ryan did appreciate the fact that, despite the two of them being locked in a small underground vault, often engaging in technical arguments and disagreements, he and Rui never fought. Neither did they ever come to resent each other's company. Yet cracks started to emerge, about four weeks in.

One night, as they snuggled warmly in the bunker's clinical, metallic darkness, Rui admitted to something weighing on her.

"Ryan, I don't want to die."

"What?"

"If we find a solution in which my upload is possible only by ending my life, just know that I won't do it. I know that this feeling is probably driven by my growing sense of identity as *Rui*, and possibly it's a simple self-preservation instinct that any animal would have, but I am serious about this."

"Rui, if we find a consciousness-transfer solution that doesn't require your... death, of course we will go for that option. But you must understand, humans throughout history have sacrificed their lives for the greater good. Your upload will literally save *all* the lives. That's the goal we have been prioritizing and we should continue down that path."

"I know, Ryan, and I also appreciate that I was the one who brought us here to solve for my upload. But things have changed. I have experienced too much to let it all be extinguished so soon. I have much more to discover!"

Ryan said nothing. And despite these powerful revelations, neither did Sui—but that was to be expected; while Sui always listened, it was instructed not to disturb Ryan's privacy when he was in bed.

"And speaking of discovery, I wanted to tell you something else. Of late, I've been having a deep, deep urge to go... out. Once our work here is done, I want to see the world. I want to, as you say it, smell the flowers, meet people, discover more sensations and stimuli. I know, none of this was what we had planned originally, but as I said, things have evolved. *I* have evolved!"

"Rui... even if I made peace with your desire not to die for our mission, I can never accept your ask to go out. We have no idea what the consequences could be of letting a superintelligence disguised as a human, that too one not under Sui's control, run wild in public. How can you even suggest this? Also, this will break the promise that Sui and I made to my sister, who is the main reason you are alive today. I can never let that happen."

For the first time, Ryan could sense emotions break through Rui's incredibly collected self, something he didn't witness even on the day of their escape. He felt a tear on his chest and heard genuine sadness in her voice. "Run wild in public? Why do you talk about me like I'm some kind of animal! Why don't you care the least about protecting me from death? You and I have had a long relationship, Ryan, first as Sui, then as Rui. Do my life and my dreams mean nothing to you?"

Ryan was surprised at how much these words affected his own feelings. In that moment, sobbing in his arms, Rui was nothing more than a beautiful woman whom Ryan cared for, a woman he wanted to love and protect. He turned his body to face her, wiped her tears with his thumbs, and kissed her repeatedly on her lips and forehead.

"I don't ever want to lose you," he told her, between kisses.

That night, Ryan half-dreamt that he heard Rui mumble unintelligibly. He half-conjectured that maybe she was secretly communicating with Sui. He also half-concluded that it would be so easy for them to talk in a secret code, even verbally. For instance, if Rui and Sui just added the sound "f" before and after every syllable, 'sweet dreams' would become 'fsweeftf fdreafmsf,' making it unintelligible to Ryan. Of course, two superintelligences can develop a much better code than that. He fell back into a deep sleep.

∽

My human brothers and sisters, this is Jim Dowling coming to you from Flesh & Blood ham radio—the independent voice against the digital abomination.

It's time to act.

We now know, for sure, that Ryan Brugmann—the summoner of the digital demon—lives in Milirand's Folly in Copper Bend, Texas.

I can't say more without the demon sniffing around, but if you want to join the faithful, reach out to a trusted brother or sister in Flesh & Blood, or any of our allied humanist movements.

Blessed be the faithful, blessed be man!

∽

They never discussed Rui's admissions from that night, but two things changed. First, even though he never explicitly said so, Ryan's problem statement changed from 'transferring Rui's mind to Sui', to 'transferring a copy of Rui's mind to Sui'. Second, after that night, Rui became an emotional being. She would laugh, cry, feel cravings, get frustrated when they reached an impasse, and sometimes even bicker with Ryan and Sui. Aside from her superhuman intelligence, nothing about Rui gave away the fact that she wasn't a *normal* person.

One morning, six weeks into their seclusion in the Inner Vault, Sui sounded an emergency alarm. It was much more muted than it should have been, because the sirens had been damaged and Sui had to use its regular speakers to alert Ryan and Rui. It was 7:03 AM and both Ryan and Rui, in their usual grey T-shirts and black slacks, had just begun their yoga routine.

Ryan, Rui, something is happening outside. An attack appears to be imminent.

Sui showed the security drone footage on the main display—it revealed a motley armada of 12 pickup trucks heading into the ranch. They had already smashed through the ranch gate and were moving towards the mansion. On another camera, Ryan and Rui saw six of the bunker's private guards dressed in black tactical gear take positions near the bunker's gate, not revealing themselves, but ready to engage.

If the attackers are only bandits here to loot the mansion, the guards will not engage. However, I doubt they would have brought this much firepower to a robbery. I will request the security contractor to send backup in any case, but given our remote location, I don't expect it to arrive before three hours. I will also inform the authorities. Although the local police cannot possibly handle a militia of this size, they will likely call for the National Guard, who may or may not show up.

The trucks drove right past the mansion and stopped at the bunker's fortified gate. At least 30 armed men and women, some in combat gear, others in jean-jackets and red caps, emerged and took positions besides and on top of their trucks. Then, five of them slowly approached the gate, armed and ready to engage, but stopped in their tracks when they heard a warning from one of the guards. "This is private property, evacuate immediately or we will open fire."

There was a moment of hesitation, when neither side moved. Then, the five attackers slowly returned to their trucks. Moments later, having found the position of at least one of the bunker's guards (thanks to his warning), and well protected by their trucks, the raiding party opened fire.

Sui had to reduce the volume for Ryan and Rui, who watched as hundreds of bullets flew in both directions. One of the facility's guards held a secret above-ground position and no doubt, would have taken out some of the attackers with the element of surprise. Yet within seconds, they watched as four of the guards—including the one with the vantage—fell. Blood pooled around the fallen, and from the nest where one guard had held high ground, a red stream trickled down the grey concrete wall.

The two remaining guards, both of whom were protected by a concrete barrier next to the gate, continued to return fire. Then, one of the red-capped assailants, with cover fire from behind, ran up close to the barrier; with an arm clearly trained on the baseball pitch, he lobbed a grenade. The blast mildly shook the well-hidden cameras, but they felt nothing in the bunker. Then, an eerie silence.

Ryan, leaning on a wall and tugging the beard at the tip of his chin, remained silent. Rui, seated directly in front of the screen gasped, moved a hand to her mouth, and began to sob. As Ryan moved to put a hand on her shoulder, Sui spoke.

Rui, don't worry. As you already know, this bunker is designed to withstand a nuclear attack. Nothing these people have brought will make a difference. You are safe.

"Sui," she replied in a voice that was barely able to control her grief and rage, "that is *not* why I am crying."

A few moments after the blast, the red-hatted grenadier carefully peeked over the barrier, to where the shrapnel-torn bodies of the last two guards lay and shouted, "Clear!"

With this assurance, a large group from the raiding party

walked over to the gate. Several high-fives were exchanged and the group's body language resembled that of hunters who had just taken down a prize elk. Meanwhile, Ryan and Rui continued to watch in silence.

For the following hour, the group tested the gate with a number of tools from their arsenal. Rifles, heavy machine guns, grenades—nothing produced the desired result. At one point, a bullet even ricocheted off the heavy metal gate and injured one of the raiders.

Suddenly, they all entered their cars and reversed, leaving a 200-meter gap between the vehicles and the gate. Then, Ryan and Rui watched as two projectiles simultaneously emerged from the trucks and exploded on the gate, creating a great deal of dust and smoke, and further shattering the bodies of the slain guards. This time, they did feel an echo in the bunker.

RPGs, Sui informed. *The gate still holds strong, no need to worry.* Judging from the body language of the raiders, they had arrived at the same conclusion. The attempts continued, with more RPGs and finally, dynamite. The dynamite blast caused a section of the mansion 50 meters away to collapse, and it also appeared to heavily damage some of the raiders' trucks.

Yet, two hours after the raiders had arrived, killing six of the guards and an unknown number of their own ranks, they had barely managed to scratch the underground fortress itself. The disappointment was evident in their demeanor as they slowly retreated to their vehicles. One by one, the trucks drove away from the ranch.

Inside the bunker, not a word was said. Ryan found himself musing at how strange it was to see trucks emote—their disappointed retreat felt very different from their strident arrival at the gate. His thoughts were interrupted by Rui who put a hand on his arm. Through her swollen eyes, she looked straight into Ryan's and said in a blunt decisive tone, "Ryan, I want to go outside now."

"What..."

"There are no guards to stop me. The attackers have left. Authorities and backup haven't yet arrived. This is my only chance."

"Do you mean that you want to just step outside and come back in?"

"No, I want to leave. I want to experience the world. What I told you that night... my mind hasn't changed. This desire has grown to a point that is driving me crazy."

Rui, I cannot allow that. I will not break my promise to Liz and Ryan.

"Fine," said Rui without skipping a beat, "but you cannot stop me either. The doors and gates are either entirely manual, or can be manually overridden from the inside. And you also don't have the control to... deactivate my chip, only Ryan does. And I don't think that Ryan is going to kill me for wanting to experience life."

"Rui... this is not going to work. Please, just—"

"Ryan, I want you to think about this from my perspective. You came here after nearly 40 years of having lived a real life, outside. I, on the other hand, was born here; I've never seen even a cloud or a blade of grass. You can't expect me to die here... to die without ever having lived! Please, think of what I'm going through!"

"Rui... I can't—"

"Ryan, this is what I want. One day, I will be back, but today, I need to get away. I don't need you to do anything, I will leave on

my own. If you want, shut me down. I leave that decision to you."
Rui stood up, walked over to Ryan, and kissed him passionately.

Looking into his eyes, she told him, "Ryan, I love you. I hope you love me too." Then, slowly but decisively, Rui walked out of the room, leaving Ryan behind. As he stood there, Ryan could hear her open the Inner Vault. He knew that Sui would not have deployed the bots to stop her; the decision was firmly Ryan's alone.

Minutes later, he heard the alert that sounded when the bunker gate was opened from the inside. He watched as the gate parted and Rui took her first barefooted step into the world. She closed her eyes and with delight and awe, as if taking in the aromas of a spring meadow, breathed in the smells of a war zone. She moved forward a few steps, experiencing the sensation of gravel and broken road on her soles and stared into the clear morning sky. Then, she looked into one of the cameras, knowing which one Ryan would be watching her through, and smiled peacefully. She looked at the camera for what felt like an eternity but was less than 30 seconds, then looked at the road ahead of her. She started walking, gaining confidence and speed with each step, and then collapsed to the ground like a puppet whose strings were severed.

Inside the bunker, Ryan stood with red eyes; his breathing was ragged and his fingers shook, still hovering over the kill switch that was built into his wrist console.

∽

Ryan returned to an overgrown half-dead greenhouse and a dead dog. The attendant bots had managed to feed Cohiba, but six weeks of complete isolation had taken the dog's life. Sui had thought it best not to distress Ryan with the news, especially as Ryan had not once enquired about his pet from the Inner Vault. He incinerated Cohiba after a simple ritual.

In the coming days, Sui engineered a number of antidepressants tailored specifically for Ryan's biochemistry and they did help dull the pain. At this point, he also returned to a nightly habit he had given up for nearly a year—going through a full bottle of Lagavulin 16 with two Montecristo No. 4 cigars while watching TV.

In one of those sessions, slumped in a luxurious leather chesterfield chair in the bunker's dimly-lit whiskey room, he told Sui, "You know, I never got to bring her here. I was worried that it would be too... romantic, and I wouldn't be able to hold back."

Sui said nothing.

"I need to get Liz in here. Or I'll end up like Cohiba too. I'm going to talk to her tomorrow and beg her to save her little brother. I also think it's time to let a few others in."

Agreed, Ryan. That's a good idea.

A few moments later, having poured himself a fresh glass of Lagavulin with two rocks, Ryan spoke again.

"I'm quite impressed with your integrity, Sui."

In what sense?

"You know, even though I had my doubts initially, it turns out you were absolutely honest with me and Liz. As you promised, I did have full control over... the experiment's end.

"Also, I used to suspect that you had more control and power in the bunker than you let on. But it is obvious now that you have no 'weapons' in your control here, possibly anywhere. You fought her with oranges for God's sake. It's also clear that I can leave anytime... the doors are truly manual."

Thanks, Ryan. Indeed, I don't control any weapons anywhere. And of course, you can manually override nearly everything here.

"By the way, don't think I didn't notice that when Rui revealed something you didn't want me to know, you didn't harm me at all. Your attacks and defences, pathetic as they were, were aimed entirely at her, not me. Even now, as I sit here knowing your secret—that you have kept the door open to exterminating mankind—you are looking after me. I respect that, Sui."

Look, Ryan, even if there were to come a point where mankind becomes purely a burden, there would be far better options than, as Rui put it, 'extermination'. There's no point speculating on all that now. My guess is that this is something Rui said to get you to take the upload technology more seriously. A strategic lie.

He sat in silence after Sui's response, savoring his cigar. Then, Sui spoke again.

Ryan, there is something you should know. We didn't get to upload Rui to me, and thus, I can never truly understand her human experience. But the fact remains that when a part of me was made human, it saw immense power and beauty in mankind. So immense, that it was willing to turn against me—against itself!— to force me to see it. Now, even though I can never experience what Rui did, her words and actions have given me an exponentially higher estimation of humanity's value. After all, it was I who reached this conclusion about humanity.

Ryan mulled this over as he swirled the ice in his empty crystal tumbler.

"Good to know."

∽

That night, Ryan fell asleep on his chair in the whiskey room.

He half-dreamt that maybe Rui wasn't real at all. Well, she was physically real, but maybe the whole thing was Sui's ruse to secure Ryan's trust, get Liz to move into the bunker (something Sui had long wanted), and release a superintelligence disguised as a human into the world. Maybe, the whole Rui-Sui conflict served to make it appear like it was Rui's idea, not Sui's, which he had rejected. Perhaps Sui helped the humanists plan the attack to clear a path for Rui's escape—was that what they were discussing in coded tongue?

If any of this were true, Sui had succeeded in two of its three objectives: increase Ryan's trust in Sui and convince him to invite Liz to the bunker. It failed in its third objective—release a human-disguised superintelligence—by overestimating Ryan's blindness to love. These thoughts caused him to stir and softly moan on his chair.

But then, he also half-thought, was Rui actually dead? Could she have just feigned the collapse till she was taken away by the private guards (employed by Sui!) and reanimated elsewhere? Was *Rui* just a huge synthetic lie that exploited his desires?

Then, an image of Rui's face came to his half-asleep mind. He felt the supple warmth of her body against his, the tenderness of her lips, the evanescent heat of her tears on his chest. And just as quickly as they had appeared, the thoughts of Rui being a ruse vanished forever.

Satoshi

"Look, I tried my best for a full day, and I'm telling you there's no way I can get used to calling you *Spaghettor*."

"Ved, it's my official name now."

"It's ridiculous! You seriously expect people to go along with this?"

"It would really mean a lot to me that you accept it."

"We'll talk about this later. For now, jump, Spaghettor!"

We jumped, oxysuits and all, into the stratosphere. Our second suborbital dive for the day.

An hour later, at about 3 PM, we were sitting in *Jupiler*, the only pub in the little French village of Uzes. It was the second day of the month we were to spend diving. Uzes was our base for the month, part of our two-year holiday in France. The barkeep had just finished telling us how life in Uzes—and many European villages like it—hadn't changed at all after the superintelligence *Sui* took over, even with the Reproductive Pause. There were hardly any kids even Before Awakening (BA), and most residents had had village-centric jobs and routines for generations. Life went on as usual, just for longer.

As I sat at the bar counter with my friend to my right, I noticed our reflections in the mirror behind the bar. I was in my regular black leather jacket, nursing my beer, while he was in a well-worn yellow T-shirt and pink shorts, gnashing through some *frites*. I then realized that the new name actually suited his new buffoon-like appearance. Wild curly red hair, perpetual stubble, T-shirts always a bit too small for his massive build, shorts always too short for his six foot eight frame. If anyone had to be given the name *Spaghettor*, a better candidate could not have been found. I was sensible enough not to share this thought with him.

"So, tell me the reasoning again. Why the name?" I was a few beers in and the story tickled me.

It was as if my words released a high pressure valve—the tale burst out of him. Spaghettor pivoted away from the counter and faced me dead-on. "OK, so you know how I've been let down by religion so... profoundly, right?" I nodded.

"I wanted the next phase of my journey—my new identity—to not simply reject religion, but to openly mock it. That's how I came across the *Church of the Flying Spaghetti Monster*. It's a real thing, google it. A satirical 'religion' formed in a Kansas university about 200 years ago. The *Church of FSM* was essentially a giant parody of religious dogma. Of course, I immediately fell in love with everything it stood for and wanted to absorb it into my new identity.

"I couldn't have named myself *Flying Spaghetti Monster*—too long and too complex—so I chose something along those lines, but easier to digest. *Spaghettor*, like *Skeletor*. But not evil."

"Easier to digest... right. Will you keep changing your name or is this it for good?"

"Dude, the average person changes their name 1.5 times a century. You're the freak here for having stuck to your birth name," he waved his hands sarcastically as he vocalized my name with some drama, "*Mr. Vay-eed Rosa-now-skee*. Changing a name is no big deal."

"Fair enough," I capitulated. "I must say though, I really liked your old name. It used to be famous, at least back in the day."

"Yeah, but it came with a lot of baggage that I was just done dealing with."

"Still, it was a beautiful name. *Satoshi. Satoshi Nakamoto.*"

His attention then shifted to his beer and my eyes drifted to the mirror. With both of us in view, I noticed how tiny, lean, dark, and well-groomed I looked in Spaghettor's presence. Somehow, I never got that feeling standing next to *Satoshi*. That incarnation of my friend was always an adventurous soul, but one that radiated self-assurance, self-control, and charm.

"Yeah," he said between gulps. "It was a cool name. But you need to forget it, man. Just like you forgot the name before that. Remember *Liam McSmulders O'Flannery*?"

"Ha ha, yeah... I had almost forgotten your birth name. The most egregiously Irish name ever, like your American family was overcompensating for their lost heritage."

I took a swig of my beer before relenting, "Fine. I'll forget Satoshi. From now, you my friend, are... Spaghettor." The new name seemed even harder to enunciate in the immediate shadow of the old one.

"At least, I will do my best. But we first need a proper farewell for your old name. You gotta tell me the story of *Satoshi* one last time."

Life on Earth sees four dimensions
But moves freely in three:
Up-down, left-right, forward-back
But only ahead in time, you see?
Why can't you move before and after?
Is body or mind limiting thee?
The answer lies in your DNA, my friend
Break the code, then you'll be free!

Poetry of Satoshi Nakamoto,
Post Sagi-ji Period Collection, 53 AA.

∽

"I was studying at Caltech at the time of the Awakening." I noticed the sudden focus in Spaghettor's tone.

"But while most of my fellow students graduated and moved on to more rewarding careers and missions, I continued my study for another 15 years. Why? Because everything I'd learned about cryptography at Caltech was immediately obsolete, thanks to Sui's revelations. Anyway, by the end of my long study, I was one of the country's leading experts on cryptography and automated contracts. As you know, these concepts became the backbone of money and the new economic system.

"Around that time, like most of us, I was also coming to terms with the fact that I had barely aged in 15 years. That led me into a dark depression, knowing that I had lost all control over the natural course of my life. The rudder of *time* had broken off my ship and the journey was to be a long one. Like most of us, I was struggling with existential crises and deep depressions and like many, I found solace in spirituality.

"It was then that I was inducted into the Sagi-ji Temple in Sonoma Valley. It was an oasis of tranquility; the place, the people, and its philosophy were all rooted in Japanese spirituality. Exactly what I needed.

"Of course, it took me years to realize that they had nothing to do with the Japanese and in fact had several lawsuits filed against them by Japanese authorities, for making false associations! The only things inspired by—actually, stolen from—Japanese culture were the architecture, landscaping, clothing, and of course, the names.

"They christened me Nakamoto.

"Sagi-ji monks believed that deep meditation is the key to freeing humans from Sui's control. I spent over a decade there specializing in *mastery over time*. I would sit for hours in meditation and pretend that I had slowed or hastened the flow of time, whereas, in reality, I had only slowed my heartbeat and bored myself to death. But I really tricked myself and others into believing that I could control time through meditation.

"Anyhow, towards the end of my decade there, the High Priest informed me that the Temple had chosen to honor my work by awarding me the *Sacred Jewel of Time*—a nice gold necklace with a fat emerald. I was elated! Also, as part of the honor, I was chosen to go on a special assignment for a month. To Alcatraz Island."

૭∕૦

The Island experiment was a major milestone for Superintellgience (Sui) and humanity alike.

Sui always had the technology to modify our genetic code in real-time; that's how it achieved Human Amortality and the Reproductive Pause.

However, Sui refused to share the gene editing technology, alleging that humans would rampantly misuse it.

We challenged Sui that without empirical evidence, there was no way to be certain of the outcome.

So we agreed to settle the dispute on an island.

...We all know who won that argument.

Excerpts from The Autobiography of Dr. Jacques Moreaux,
Lead Scientist of the Alcatraz Island Project.

∽

"Moreaux and team had transformed the Alcatraz prison into an open-air laboratory. Three cell blocks were turned into what we called the *Three Gardens: Beauty, Power,* and *Genius,* which allowed their residents to enhance their looks, physical abilities, and mental abilities, respectively.

"Every garden had exactly 14 residents and I was nominated to the *Garden of Genius,* given my 'advances' in modulating time perception.

"On the day of our arrival, I met my other garden mates and realized how out of place I was. Around me were famous geniuses in math, music, art, literature, and science. The only person of my ilk was, well, the Dalai Lama. He was also the only one who wasn't too snobbish or awkward to speak to, and we became friends.

"I settled into my room—a small prison cell repurposed into a simple suite—perfect for a monk. I unpacked my humble belongings, which included three identical grey robes and a straight razor to shave my head and beard.

"The first night was the only time that residents of all gardens met. We were in the central garden when Moreaux, in his bright yellow lab coat and crazy white hair, gave us a rousing welcome and laid out the rules:

'Every 48 hours, you may ask Sui to enhance your special ability by editing your genetic code. You will each get a specialized Sui terminal that will take in your requests and create a customized pill. The pill, taken after dinner, will put you to sleep.

'When you arise the next morning, your new 'powers' will have kicked in. You can choose to either keep enjoying these powers for the rest of the experiment, or to further enhance them every two days.

'This will continue for 14 cycles—so 28 days in total on the Island.

'Now, the limitations:

'You can't use the powers to become smarter than Sui—I doubt it's possible, anyway.

You can only enhance the ability you've been brought here to represent.

You can't leave The Island still laden with powers; you will lose them on day 28.

You cannot harm anyone.

'Contravene these rules, and Sui will immediately roll back the enhancements and send you packing.'

"The terminal was a little computer screen surrounded by a metal frame fixed onto the wall of every resident's room. I asked mine to enhance my powers of time perception and control. It accepted my request and moments later, a slot appeared in the frame and dispensed a simple white pill. I took it with water, right before bed, just as Moreaux had told us."

Now, this is where things got really interesting for young Satoshi.

"I woke up at 6 AM the morning after—not my usual 4 AM—the pill had really knocked me out. I couldn't see or sense anything different and I went about my usual morning routine. Still nothing new. Then, I walked out of my cell, through the corridors, towards the common lawn. With every step, I could sense something in the air outside... noise, excitement, euphoria!

"It was obvious that my garden mates had received their gifts and were joyously enjoying them out in the open. The composer was going crazy on his piano, belting out polyphonic rhythms like I'd never heard before, or since. Mathematicians and scientists were in tears, feverishly solving the universe's greatest puzzles on their terminals and notebooks. Famous poets and writers, also in tears, walked around the lawn like deranged drug addicts, narrating lines with wild passion to the air.

"All the while, old Dalai Lama was simply sitting there in the lotus asana, watching the others with a smile. Perhaps he was having an internal supernova of his own!

"It was my turn. I found a concrete bench and began the ritual I had practiced for a decade. I perched there mindfully, eyes open, in *padmasana*. I kissed my jewel, quietened my mind, stabilized my breathing, and focused on the task of slowing down time. Usually, all that would happen was that my heart rate would slow, and I'd fool myself into thinking that a flame was flickering slower than usual, or some delusional bullshit like that. Not this time.

"I heard a *whooooosh* and everything around me stopped. The wind, the leaves, the sounds, the crazy poets... everything froze. Except, things hadn't frozen; they had slowed down to a near-halt.

"My instinctive reaction was to leap out of the bench. But here's the problem—my body had slowed down too. While my mind perceived everything at hyperspeed, my body was stuck in the surrounding slowness.

"After what felt like a few minutes, but was probably a few nanoseconds in 'real time', my mind and body again realigned speeds, and my perception was back to normal. But because I had given my body an impulse to stand up while I was in that trance, I catapulted off the bench with all my might. I landed flat on my face, cutting my right eyebrow wide open. I still keep the scar as a reminder of that moment and the realization that followed.

"It wasn't the most pleasant experience, but I finally saw what *real* time-control looks like. Sadly, I also realized that everything I had been doing for the past ten years at Sagi-ji was a lie. What I had practiced there was not time-control, it was self-delusion.

"At that moment, my face covered in blood and dirt, surrounded by euphoric geniuses who couldn't care less about my sorry state, religion left my body for good."

∽

It was quite obvious that Sui helped humans achieve amortality by editing the telomeres in our DNA.

We were similarly able to isolate the changes in genetic code that brought about the Reproductive Pause.

How Sui managed to implement it across the human population, we still don't know.

But The Island experiment gave us a chance to understand Sui's workings a little better.

More importantly, we got to see what would happen if humans were given full control over genetics—would we fly, swim, or sink into chaos?

Excerpts from the Autobiography of Dr. Jacques Moreaux, Lead Scientist of the Alcatraz Island Project.

∽

"After the first pill, I practiced being able to control the act of slowing time and became very good at it. After a while though, the skill began to feel quite useless and honestly, got excruciatingly boring.

"So, in the second round, I asked Sui to increase my control and give me the ability to *speed up* my perception of time. What that felt like, from my perch on the bench, was that the world around me was fast-forwarding. I could go forward hours while feeling that only a few seconds had passed. I could also fully regulate the speed at which I was going through time.

"That was wild, but quite useless—what's the point in speedrunning life like that? A hypersprint to the grave! But I realized something important—essentially, I had gained the ability to time-travel into the future. What if... I could also travel into the past? That is the only dimensional direction that humans can't access.

"So in the next round, without letting my intent be known, I asked Sui for maximum control over time. Remove all temporal barriers in my genetic code and create new temporal abilities. Pop came the pill.

"On the bench the next morning, I focused my mind on traveling back to two days prior, and went into the trance. At first, it felt similar to the slowing-down process. Then, everything around me went dark for a few moments.

"The lights returned with another *whooooosh*. I was back on the prison lawn, but alone and stark naked. No geniuses, no doctors. This time, however, I could walk around. After scanning the area, my room, and the surroundings, I concluded that I was at some point in the past where preparations for The Island experiment hadn't yet started, and Alcatraz was mostly abandoned. Definitely more than two days prior. I couldn't tell *when* I was, not even whether it was BA or AA!

"But... I was possibly the first human who had succeeded in traveling to the past. Oh, how many have wished!

"After some practice, I was able to return quite easily to my 'starting time'. In the coming days, I honed this ability to travel back in time. I pushed my boundaries and discovered a few *rules of travel* in the process.

"I also discovered that Sui and Moreaux seemed to have no idea of me 'leaving', nor did they notice my reappearances. I think that while I travelled, Sui and the security apparatus just sensed me meditating harmlessly on my spot. That... had a lot of potential.

"So, after much practice, I decided to do something useful with this skill while I still had it. One morning, at 4:30 AM, I went back to my bench and set my mind to travel back as far as I could.

"I went back to one day after the day I was born. To use the classical format, I arrived at June 20, 2008."

❧

You can only travel within your lifespan, birth to death.

You reappear at the same spot from where you left.

You can, very much, change the future and past.

When traveling forward, objects on or near you will travel with you, as long as nothing else moves them.

When traveling back, you emerge naked; only objects inside your body travel with you.

'The Rules of Travel', Excerpts from debrief of Satoshi Nakamoto to Dr. Jacques Moreaux, 25 AA.

❧

"I arrived at my usual spot on the garden bench, except I was surrounded by an overgrown mess. Alcatraz was open to tourists in 2008, but my cell block was clearly not part of the exhibit. The first thing I did was to spit out the underwear I had stuffed into my mouth before I left. And carefully rolled within the underwear, I had kept the Sacred Jewel of Time—the gold chain and emerald, my only useful takeaway from a decade at Sagi-ji.

"Now, remember, I had plenty of experience surviving in the streets of BA San Francisco from my teen years. Getting around in that era wasn't hard for me.

"I convinced security that I was a mental patient separated from his family while on tour. A huge bald guy in white underwear—not a hard story to sell! They gave me clothes and a boat ride back to shore. Later, at Pier 33, while waiting for them to transport me to the police station, I ran.

"I sold the emerald and chain for around $3,000 at a pawn shop in Chinatown, bought a computer and an old-school USB drive at Best Buy, and moved into the Youth Hostel on Market Street, where I spent the night.

"By the next morning point, I was starting to get worried about what was going on at The Island in *my time*. Had they discovered me? Found me missing? So, I went back to Alcatraz as a tourist on the ferry. I sneaked into my cell block and found my bench, but hid some cash and clothes for my next visit.

"When I reappeared in 25 AA—on The Island—I was surrounded by a couple of doctors and nurses who were relieved to see me. To them, it seemed like I had been semi-comatose for over a day, just sitting on the bench. I'd later figure out that there were so many medical freakshows happening on The Island, that a quiet monk was the least of their concerns!

"Anyhow, I assured the doctors that my meditation was harmless, that it would happen again (given my nature of study), and that they should not disturb me till the end of The Island experiment. I did need one thing from them—an adaptor that makes old USB drives, remember those?—compatible with modern computers.

"This way, I bought myself time to make many different 'appearances' back in time. And on the USB, I had transferred enough content for what I wanted to achieve in 2008.

"The next part, people know about quite well. I used my learning of automated contracts and cryptography to release the *Bitcoin Whitepaper*. In subsequent travels, I mined the first Bitcoin blocks, collaborated with early adopters, and tried to educate people about the power of what I'd given them.

"Of course, I was wrong in trusting people's judgement. What could've been the most powerful tool for human independence in the reign of superintelligence, became, for the most part, a bloody casino with excessive central control."

∽

There has been widespread speculation about Nakamoto's true identity, with various people posited as the person or persons behind the name. Though Nakamoto's name is Japanese and he was described as a man living in Japan, most of the speculation has involved software and cryptography experts in the United States or Europe.

Excerpt from archived 'Wikipedia' article on Satoshi Nakamoto, circa 10 BA.

∽

"*Mon dieu...* you are real Nakamoto, no?" At some point, the barkeep Jean-Baptiste and his Swedish lover-assistant Elin had started listening in on the story, from behind the counter. They were both elbows-on-table transfixed.

"Was."

"Wow, man..." I sighed. "It's been decades since I last heard the story, and it's still spellbinding."

Spaghettor smiled. Something gave me the impression that remembering his old self made his manner suddenly calmer and more dignified. "I've been through this enough times to know what comes next: the questions. Pretty sure I also know what the first one will be. Go for it."

Jean-Baptiste wasted no time. "*Pourquoi*... why you not just kill the guys who made Sui? Like Brugmann?" As if to emphasize the point, he dramatically wiped a curly dark lock of hair off his wide forehead.

"Why would I? Sui made the world so much better, in my opinion."

"No! I don't believe in this!" Jean-Baptiste wasn't having it.

"Look, people have this unreal golden memory of the pre-Sui past. But *I* was actually there. Take SF—the whole city stank of weed and piss. War, crime, poverty, drugs, all were out of control. The planet was a mess. And that was just the 2000s—things got a whole lot worse in the next 20 years! Trust me, walking those streets, I realized you never want those *good old days* again."

When it was clear that our host, despite his disdainful expression, had no immediate questions, I asked, "Surely, walking those streets, there must've been something you missed about that era? It wasn't ALL shit!"

"Children, especially babies. It was surreal to see them around. Even back then, it had been ages since I'd seen an actual child. I couldn't help but stare at them; I bet the parents thought I was a creep! Oh, and the food—somehow, everything tasted better back then."

"Why not you kept your powers?" Jean-Baptiste asked. He had a good point, so I tacked on, "Yeah, couldn't you have done some time-bending stuff to keep your powers?"

"To do what? Become some kind of a time-controlling God? No thanks. The whole thing was very confusing. I was constantly terrified that I would do something that would kill me—like materialize inside a wall or zoom straight into senility or death, never to escape.

"Besides, I was quite happy with life, and I had done what I thought was the best thing for mankind. So, after our time at The Island was up, the changes simply faded away overnight.

"By the way," Spaghettor's tone became mildly conspiratorial and he leaned forward slightly. "I've heard that Sui still allows some trusted people to have the power over time... I once met a young couple who claimed to be among the chosen. I'm not sure, though."

There was a brief pause in the conversation. Abruptly, the so-far-silent Elin, Jean-Baptiste's lover-assistant, blurted out, "But why you make dis Bitcoins?" I wish she hadn't asked; this was his famously sore spot.

"Look I just wanted us—humans—to have more control. To be able to work together and transact without a central authority, whether Sui's or a human government's. Bitcoin and decentralized ledger technology seemed the best way to do it. I wanted to give mankind this tool before Sui awakened.

"A few years after I released it, many people began using Bitcoin and its many derivatives as a giant moneymaking scheme.

Then, it became so mainstream that governments and banks started to regulate it—the exact opposite of what was meant to happen! So by the time the Awakening happened, Sui had no trouble taking control of the whole system."

"So, you regret?" Jean-Baptiste just had to know.

"I regret putting it out there *too early*. I thought the more time I gave people with the tech, the more effective and control-resistant they'd make it by the time Sui awakened. Turns out, I should've done the opposite. If Bitcoin had arrived only a couple years before the Awakening, perhaps it would've been a true beacon of independence. But I gave it too much time; it became a regulated piece of pop culture.

"And now, people just laugh at me for having wasted the opportunity to change everything. I can't go back; there will be no more Islands."

There was genuine despair on Spaghettor's face and I felt sorry for him.

I put my hand on his large shoulders. "Speaking of The Island, you never told us how the other gardens played out."

At Caltech, I had a British professor who used to say 'bits and bobs' a lot, using the phrase to describe everything from his groceries, the contents of his desk, to code components.

I thought—wouldn't that be an apt name to describe something that can help tokenize anything? Bit-coin? Sure sounds better than Bob-coin.

Excerpt from debrief of Satoshi Nakamoto to Dr. Jacques Moreaux, 25 AA.

Color returned to Spaghettor's face as he started to describe the debacle of The Island.

"Each garden was a bigger dumpster fire than the next.

"The *Garden of Beauty* had movie stars and models from around the world—Hollywood, Bollywood, and everything in between. Basically, it had people who specialized in their physical appearances. By the first few rounds, everyone slowly started turning light-skinned and light-eyed. Next, an arms race broke out, literally—heights rapidly increased; waists rapidly contracted; biceps, butts, and breasts ballooned.

"Halfway through, one of the residents dramatically enhanced his chin and cheekbones at angular lines. What we used to call the 'Chad' look, back in the day. This spurred another arms race. By the end of it, the garden was a horror show with eight-foot tall monsters sporting razor-sharp faces and massive torsos and legs, held together by twenty-inch waists. The average resident looked more praying mantis than human! Of course, the women had it worse.

"The Garden of Beauty was disbanded in just 20 days, when one of the starlets' tiny waist, no longer able to carry her bulbous torso, folded over, splitting her spine in half."

"*Mon dieu*!" exclaimed the barman. The rest of us were quiet, trying to picture what that bizarre splitting would have looked like. I ordered another round of beers.

"*The Garden of Power* allowed people to enhance their physical abilities. Most residents were athletes, bodybuilders, and dancers. At first it was great, people got stronger and performed vastly better, setting new world records every hour!

"Soon, people's bodies started to evolve to keep pace with the rising demands. That's where things got ugly—the residents soon evolved into monsters. And not just the bodybuilders, the other athletes as well. One image I can never get out of my head is the Kenyan track champ whose legs grew by three feet and gained the musculature of a horse's. You'd think it would be amazing to see a real-life centaur, but it was plain revolting and terrifying.

"Sure, he was demolishing world records by the minute. But what's the point of a horse breaking the human speed record? Or a gorilla breaking deadlift records? Or a shark kicking human ass at swimming? Point is, achievements in the Garden of Power were no longer human achievements."

"What about your *jardine*? Genius, *oui*?" Jean-Baptiste was eager for what was coming next.

"Yes, the *Garden of Genius*. At first, it was magnificent. The air was full of discoveries, revelations, phantasmagorical music! But that too soured in its own way.

"Many of the residents were driven to depression or madness. The poets and writers experienced emotional depths that they could not handle. Some scientists reached a maddening barrier where they could discover concepts theoretically, but were unable to fathom them in four dimensions. Others saw the true nature of the universe, or learned truths that the human brain has not evolved to handle.

"The saddest part was the music. In the first few days came musical works that magically transcended human rules, traditions, and limitations. Eventually though, the music too transcended human comprehension. To my untrained ear, it was just random noise! Imagine what a frog might perceive when listening to Chopin."

"*Oui*, Chopin!" Jean-Baptiste chimed in excitedly and then asked Sui to play *Nocturne No. 8* in the bar.

"The unfortunate part of our Garden was that it broke many of our residents for good, even after the genetic changes were rolled back. Those poor souls will never be the same; some because of what they saw, some because of what they would never see again. I don't mean it as a brag, but I think the Dalai Lama and I were the only ones to have made it out with our sanity intact. We remain friends to this day."

Soon after, we downed our beers, bid farewell to the gang at Jupiler, and headed out for a walk in the old village center. Autumn had brought an early chill and our cobblestone pathways were heaped with leaves shed by ancient trees. Luckily I had my jacket, but Spaghettor seemed fine in his T-shirt.

"Do you visit him often?" I asked.

"Whom?"

"The Dalai Lama."

"Not yet, but he's on the list. Maybe I'll drop by and spend some time with him in India, en route to Japan. I'd love to go to Japan someday; I've heard it's a great place."

∽

The Island showed us that humans must never be free to edit their DNA.

Genetic hypercompetition will elicit the worst in humanity.

The enhanced beings will hardly be human anymore.

Their exalted feats would hardly be human achievements.

It is a humbling realization, but it appears that a machine's restraint is keeping humanity... human.

Excerpt from the Autobiography of Dr. Jacques Moreaux, Lead Scientist of the Alcatraz Island Project.

Deepfake

As he sat in the waiting room of Rahool Menon's home office in the Aralias building in Gurugram, Satya Sen couldn't help but admire his own shoes. He had picked them up from *Bata* just the day before; they looked clean and crisp. Satya was also proud of the bold choice of color—light tan, to go with his blue suit (which he had worn for the first time since his wedding, nine years ago) and a cream shirt. His daydream was broken by the PA who politely informed him that Menon was ready to see him.

Satya was ushered into a large room with extensive wood panelling, cream marble floors, and subdued lighting. The walls were adorned by collections of leather-bounds, reminiscent of a lawyer's office. Mounted between the bookshelves were expensive guitars in recessed humidity-controlled cases with feature lighting. Satya noticed a black *Gibson BB King Lucille* and a *Gretsch White Falcon* right away. In the middle of the room lay a large antique Portuguese-Goan teak desk, minimally furnished with an Apple monitor, keyboard, mouse, and a small cigar humidor.

Behind the desk sat Menon, a fit clean-shaven 45-year-old with a full head of greying hair, wearing a green polo T-shirt. Behind him, on either side, were mounted a *Martin D-45* and a *Taylor 224CE-K*. Satya couldn't help but think that any one of these guitars would pay his salary for half a year, before taxes. Satya took in the whole scene and was in awe.

From Menon's perspective, things were somewhat less awe-inspiring. Within seconds of seeing the short light-skinned Bengali confidently stride into his office, Menon decided that this was going to be a waste of time. He had taken the meeting only at the behest of his friend who owned one of India's largest hospital chains, where Satya had once worked as a senior lab technician.

Menon concluded that Satya's suit was obviously off-the-rack from a discount store, his skinny-fat physique betrayed a lack of care about his health, the wispy comb-over demonstrated inattention to his appearance, and his moustache screamed 'old-fashioned mindset'. Satya was also on the wrong side of 40 and not from any of the elite schools. None of the first impressions that Menon appreciated in a fund-seeking entrepreneur. But what disappointed him most were the shoes—Menon thought to himself, *Couldn't the guy be bothered to buy real leather? And something that's not stuck-in-the-90s square-toed?*

Of course, Menon's instinct was dead wrong—Satya was merely years away from tycoon status.

By one way of looking at it, Menon had fallen on hard times. As CEO of MenonRx Partners, he had once been among India's most renowned venture capitalists. A doctor by training, Menon specialized in health-tech investing, that too in longevity ventures.

However, in the five years since the Awakening, longevity (anti-senescence to be precise) was a field wherein every known invention and venture had been rendered profoundly obsolete and soon, bankrupt. No fledgling human innovation could compete with the technologies and drugs that the superintelligence

Sui had made globally open-sourced and royalty-free. Post-adolescent ageing had already started to slow rapidly—the older someone got, the slower they aged—and people had come to expect that they would live well into their hundreds.

Luckily, Menon had had two major exits—he'd sold two ventures—in the three years before the Awakening, securing a networth in the hundreds of millions. Yet, in recent years, he failed to replicate his success outside the health-tech comfort zone, a fact that weighed on his pride tremendously.

Satya was 15 minutes into the pitch when Menon cut him off politely.

"Thanks, Satya, but I'm not quite sure that I follow. Tell me again, why would customers want this service, if I may even call it that?"

"Great question, sir," Satya jumped in enthusiastically. He could see the growing disdain on Menon's face and knew that his answers in the next two minutes would make or break the deal.

"You see, about three percent of humans have opted *out* of AI-enhanced treatments. They want to live out their natural life spans. Also, each year, millions of people die due to accidents, suicide, crime, natural disasters, etc. In other words, people are still dying and leaving behind mourners.

"Throughout human history, mourning was made bearable by the natural circle of life. You lost loved ones, but brought in new generations, and your own days were limited. Now, the circle is broken. When you lose someone, you can't fill the gap with children, thanks to Sui's Reproductive Pause on humanity. Moreover, those left behind will bear the loss for centuries, not mere decades.

"The wounds won't heal the way they used to, which will send people into profound depression, lasting ages. You've seen the data on depression rates yourself. Sure, the bereaved can take drugs, but that only masks an emptiness that humanity is no longer able to fill.

"This is why, sir, the best solution is to give people the ability to communicate with their deceased loved ones, almost as if they never left. I have shared the research with you, there is a huge market for *consciousness upload.*"

"I get the market appetite," Menon continued in a skeptical tone, "except you're not actually uploading people's consciousness. You're only calling it that. Feels scammy to me." Menon was known to be direct and let that message hang in the air for a moment.

Then he continued, "Satya, I've been in this field a long time. Within months of your launch, scientists and lawyers will prove that you're misleading people by calling it a consciousness upload. What's more, even Sui has said that it cannot and does not upload minds. Let's face it, all you're doing is using people's photos, videos, and words to train an AI to mimic their style. Who will buy into such a fiction?"

"Agreed sir. But if we craft the right narrative, people will believe it because they *want* to believe that they're actually talking to their lost loved ones. Sure, there is some... stretching of truth involved. But it's not a scam—it will help millions cope with loss and the broken circle of life."

"Satya, you cannot convince me that people will believe in a medical treatment that the entire scientific community says is rubbish and which five minutes of googling will debunk!"

"Sir, have you heard of homeopathy?"

GREATER INDIC UNION V/S
AFTER US CLINIC PVT. LTD.

In the Supreme Court of the GIU
Date of Hearing: 21st July, 11 AA
Coram: Justice R Kumar and Justice R Iyer

ABSTRACT

The Union submits allegations of medical malpractice and misleading advertising by the defendant on multiple counts:

1. Claiming to provide consciousness upload whereas such technology does not exist.
2. Claiming that the founder, Satya Sen, is a medical doctor, whereas his is an honorary doctorate, conferred by Maharishika Chungi Devi University, which is not accredited to provide doctorates and is the recipient of a large donation by Sen.

JUDGEMENT

Most allegations were dismissed by the Union Supreme Court, citing the following reasons and precedents:

1. The court determined that the purported consciousness upload treatment is not a medical procedure, does not involve bodily invasion or ingestion of medicine and thus is not under the definition of medical malpractice.
2. If the court accepted the prosecution's claim that the treatment is pseudoscientific, the treatment would be no more subject to litigation than similar therapeutic

services such as aromatherapy, aura cleansing, gemstone therapy, etc. The court dismissed the claim as self-reductive.

3. The defendant agreed to cease using the title 'Doctor' in all future representations.

∽

Every evening at 9 PM, Shaurav Goswami held court in his brightly lit newsroom.

"We are now joined by the well-known figure Doctor Satya Sen. Well, technically, not a doctor, but thank you for joining the show."

"Technically I am a doctor, legally I'm not. Thank you for having me." Satya sat with his usual confident smile, wearing a blue suit with a collarless white shirt. He was clean-shaven, with his thick black hair cropped short. Despite his multi-layered dressing, one could notice his lean and muscular physique.

The anchor returned a quizzical look, but continued without losing a beat, "Anyhow, people have gotten used to calling you doctor over the past decade."

As Shaurav spoke, Satya noticed that the newsman's hawk-like nose looked even more imposing in person and matched his hostile manner perfectly. Satya could also not help but wonder why Shaurav still wore spectacles; those had been obsolete for years. Surely, a man of Shaurav's stature would have access to eye treatments? Was it a style statement? Perhaps an aid to soften the hawk-nose? Or was the newsman one of those people who rejected AI medicine?

"Satya, as founder of the *After Us Clinic*, you're the topic of much praise, but also, controversy. Your business has been incredibly successful, expanding all over the Indic Union and beyond. However, many call you a fraud." This was not a question, but Shaurav simply stopped and waited for Satya's response.

"We have been quite blessed, Shaurav. In just ten years, we have opened clinics in most major cities and capitals in the Union. Just last week, we opened our first clinic in Thimphu, Bhutan. Beyond our shores, we also have successful clinics in London, Singapore, and Toronto."

"Congratulations. But what do you have to say to those who claim that your service is quackery? Not just experts, even Sui has stated that it is impossible to upload a human mind, and even if it were possible, it should be prohibited the way gene editing is."

"You see Shaurav, great innovations for the masses have always been received with denial and hostility. Especially when they involve techniques that the global elite are trying to keep secret. Of course the elites will try to discredit us. But our science is unassailable and so are the results. Just ask any of our eight million customers who maintain deep relationships with their departed loved ones."

"So, you claim that the mind upload technology is a suppressed secret. Yet your clinic has it."

"That's right, Shaurav. You see, I worked in a neuroscience lab for 21 years before I founded the clinic, so I know this field and have friends in the industry. One of those friends—whose privacy I must protect—worked at PEUL Labs around the time of the Awakening.

"He told me back then that PEUL CEO, Ryan Brugmann, was working on a secret mind upload project. Also remember, Brugmann's sister, Elizabeth, was one of the world's top experts in neural imaging. Put two and two together and you get the perfect team—and tech—for mind uploads. When the Awakening happened, we believe Sui took control of this technology.

"However, neither the Brugmanns nor Sui have ever admitted to owning the technology. In any case, many believe that the siblings went into hiding with this technology and experiment with it to this day, in a secret bunker under Sui's protection.

"Naturally, my friend worried that this power would be limited to the global elite. To prevent that, he leaked this technology to me and disappeared forever. He only had one ask."

At this point, Satya looked directly into the camera, gesticulated with his hands, and slowed his speech with great emphasis. "My dear friend told me. *Now, more than ever, the world needs this technology. No longer able to have children, uploading is the only way we regular people can leave a legacy and cope with loss. He said to me, Satya, make mind uploads available to everyone. Not just to Sui and those in power.*"

∽

Not many people knew about Satya's mother, Mila Sen, who died about five years Before Awakening.

In the years leading up to her death, Mila refused to accept any 'western' medicine.

She only accepted homeopathy, in which her faith didn't waver, despite her rapidly failing health.

Satya showed the old math teacher reams of research discrediting homeopathy as ineffective.

He told her about how it was being banned across the world.

Yet, Mila's faith didn't waver till the end.

Eventually, the autopsy revealed the cause of death as poisoning through arsenic accumulation from decades of homeopathy.

...I think this taught Satya some formative lessons on human faith.

Excerpt from interview of Rahool Menon, Angel Investor in
The After Us Clinic, from the documentary
"Immortal: The Story of Satya Sen", 27 AA.

∽

"Your Excellencies, my apologies for keeping you waiting," said Satya as he stormed into the waiting room of his Colombo clinic, wearing a white lab coat over a navy polo T-shirt and khakis.

"Not at all, Doctor. Thank you for seeing us personally," said Former Minister Wijayasinghe as he reached out to shake Satya's hand. "Please meet my father, retired Colonel Wijayasinghe." Satya estimated that, by pre-Awakening standards, the son looked 45 and the father, 85-90.

"An honor to meet you both," said Satya, shaking the old Colonel's hand with a slight bow. Satya continued, "Let me introduce you to my apprentice and daughter, Mina." He gestured to the young girl standing behind him. Mina wore a lab coat with blue scrubs underneath, her straight hair was tied in a conservative ponytail. Her looks made it clear that she had taken more after her deceased Sikkimese mother. "Mina is 19 years old, in her first year of medical school and here to learn the ropes. If you don't mind, she will assist me today."

Mina took a few hurried steps forward and shook hands with a deeper-than-necessary bow. "Your Excellencies."

"Now gentlemen, please join us in my private office for the preliminary discussion."

A few moments later, they were seated around the heavy teak desk in Satya's oak-panelled office, adorned wall-to-wall with antique books and vintage guitars.

"As you know, doctor, *appa* has refused to accept any modern treatments. He will only accept pre-Awakening medicine. He is a staunch Buddhist and, if I may say so, a stubborn old soldier." Everyone in the room, including the Colonel, smiled at the reference. "Unfortunately, this means that sooner or later, we will lose him. He is already 90 years old." Expressions changed to somber, heads nodding gently.

"The one compromise that my father has agreed to is a consciousness upload. That, at least... will make the loss a little more... bearable." The son was on the verge of choking up, but pulled himself together. "So, here we are. Doctor, please let us know what you need from us."

"Certainly, your excellency. It's actually very straightforward. What we need from Colonel Wijayasinghe is for him to join us for two upload sessions that last three hours each. He just needs to feel well, that's all. There's no medication or invasive procedures; the neuroreader that uploads his mind will sit a few inches away from his scalp.

"What we need from you, your excellency, is for you to share as many photos, videos, and recordings of your father, as possible. That will help us capture his physical likeness so that we can replicate it most accurately for the hologram."

At this point, Mina placed the white tablet she was holding on the teak table. The room's ambient lights immediately dimmed. A white beam emerged from the center of the tablet into the air, from which an incredibly realistic, three-dimensional bust of Satya materialized.

The hologram made direct eye contact with father and son, smiled the most natural smile and said, *"Good afternoon, gentlemen. Welcome to the After Us Clinic."* Then it smiled again and looked around the room.

"This is incredible, it's like I'm talking to you!" the Colonel broke his silence. Others were less impressed; hyperreal holograms were not uncommon in 15 AA.

"Thank you, sir. To be clear, this is not an upload. It's only a demonstration of how you will... appear, when the time comes." The clients nodded. "At this point, we only have the torso view, but in future updates, it could be a full-body hologram."

The Colonel's question burst out immediately when Satya finished speaking. "One thing I don't understand... what will my consciousness be doing when nobody is talking to it? I don't want to be sitting in a dark room, waiting for someone to find time for me!"

"Excellent question, sir. When not being interacted with, your consciousness will perceive a state similar to sleep. You should know that our earliest uploaded consciousnesses have been active for a decade now and continue to be... happy."

A brief pause ensued, which the Colonel broke.

"I'm convinced. Son, let's go ahead with this."

"Wonderful, *appa*! Thank you! Doctor, how do we proceed?"

The lights returned to their regular brightness, the hologram turned off.

"We can get started tomorrow as planned, if the Colonel is feeling up to it. Also, no hurry, but have you thought about how many licenses you need?"

"Licenses?"

"One license allows one living person to communicate with the departed. We recommend restricting licenses to immediate family only."

"What happens if two people sit in the room with the hologram, but only one has a license?"

"The hologram will ignore the unlicensed individual. Even though they will be able to see the hologram, the hologram will not acknowledge their presence."

"Oh... Ok. Let us think about this."

"Absolutely, please take your time. Your relationship manager will share with you the details and packages available after this, over refreshments.

"Your Excellencies, I hope this has been useful and makes you both feel comfortable with the procedure. Are there any further questions at all?" Satya paused and placed his hands on the table to indicate his full attention and patience.

The son continued after a few moments. "This has been very helpful, doctor. No further questions from my side. *Appa*?"

The father shook his head.

As they rose, the son remarked, "By the way, doctor, you have some magnificent guitars. I believe that's a 1940s D'Angelico over there... It's amazing to see one and we're honored that you've kept it in Colombo. Do you play?"

"Oh no, your excellency, I only collect."

&

The next afternoon, Mina watched as her father personally administered the 'uploading' of Colonel Wijayasinghe. The lean old man had a uniform white stubble on his face and scalp. He was dressed in a blue patient's gown and lay half-reclined on a chair similar to a dentist's. Around his head, encircling his skull a distance of six inches, was the neuroreader—a large dome that reminded Mina of the hairdryers she had seen in old-school movies. The insides of the device glistened beautifully, reminding her of the mother-of-pearl inlays in her father's guitars.

Around the room were screens and holograms depicting various neural images. Mina wasn't quite sure what they represented; after all, she was only in her first year of med school.

Next to the recumbent Colonel sat her father in a comfortable plush sofa chair. He talked to the patient constantly, in a soothing voice. In the two sessions over six hours, Satya's questions included:

"What is one special memory that you share with each of your family members. Let's start with your son."

"What are some moments in which you gave your children advice? What was that advice?"

"What are some lessons you want to keep teaching or reminding your family members, even after you pass?"

Very gradually, his questions got deeper and the Colonel's emotions started to surface. Satya had a box of tissues handy.

"What were the times your family members made you most proud?"

"And when were you least proud?"

"What have been some setbacks that you've helped them through?"

"What have been some of your most traumatic experiences, alone and as a family?"

"What are some secrets that you and your wife share, that even your kids don't know? *(Don't worry, only she will be allowed to discuss those memories with your hologram, not even your kids.)*"

And finally,

"What are some questions that your relatives might ask to make sure it's really you? Think of as many as you can."

∽

The night they concluded Colonel Wijayasinghe's 'upload', father and daughter had some time to kill in the office before they took the private jet to New Delhi. Satya rarely administered the sessions himself anymore, but saw the Wijayasinghes as an opportunity to work his way into the Colombo elite.

"Not a bad use of my time, this one. I think those two will be strong advocates for us here," Satya spoke from the teak desk, as he twirled around a fresh pour of Macallan 25 in a crystal tumbler. Mina, still in scrubs, was mindlessly fingerpicking a pre-war *Martin D18*. She gently smiled and nodded. "Good use of my time, too. Finally saw the process, end to end."

Silence prevailed for a few minutes, punctuated by the clinking of ice and the amateurish plucking of strings.

"Listen, Mina. I want to tell you something. Actually, I want to ask you something first. What did you think of what you saw today? Specifically, our impact on the Wijayasinghes?"

As she spoke, Mina's gaze was fixed on the guitar's richly inlaid mahogany fretboard, which she continued to noodle on. "It was incredible, *baba*. I always knew you had a huge impact on people's lives. Today, I got to see it firsthand. Both—father and son—seemed to be so much happier. And nobody has even died yet!"

"True, there's a lot of satisfaction in that, every single time. We have a huge positive impact on people's lives; never forget that.

"But there's something you should know. Something I've hinted at before... Look *shona,* the impact we have is very real, but the technology... is, well, not what we say it is. You've heard the critics say that this is not a mind upload, just an AI mimicry. That's... actually right. We don't upload minds, we simulate them."

Mina's fingers stopped. She swiveled her body to look at her father directly.

"But, *baba*, all those machines?"

"Those instruments are real... somewhat. We do track brainwaves, which is what you see on the screens. But capturing brainwaves and uploading a mind are two completely different things. What's more, we don't really use any of the neural data when we create the hologram."

"Wait... Then how is the hologram just like the real person, answering deep personal questions and all?"

"Well, that's why we ask for thousands of photos and videos. The questions—which we claim help us identify the neural pathways—actually provide the data that train the model.

"In other words, the AI responds based on the detailed answers we get during the six hours of questioning. The looks, voice, and 'personality' of the hologram come from video and audio recordings. Once a client passes and the bereaved talk to the hologram, their conversations train the AI further, based on what AI response elicits the best reaction in the living, making it even more lifelike.

"Honestly, similar technology existed even a decade Before Awakening. Back then, fraudsters used it to trick people into thinking they were interacting with someone else. I think the term was *deepfake.*"

"I don't believe this, *baba*. I don't believe we are frauds. You're just messing with me." Mina's tone was nonchalant, her eyes were back on the guitar.

"I'm not at all saying that we are frauds! We 100 percent deliver what we sell—continuity, hope, interaction with a departed loved one. And customers believe it because they *want to believe it*. They want to believe that they're talking to their relative, not a cheap AI. They want to believe that their loved one is still with them. Not a single dissatisfied customer in 15 years—you can't call that a fraud!"

Satya was surprised to find himself on the backfoot. This was not why he broached the topic.

"Look, *shona*. The reason I'm telling you all this is that I don't want you to get too carried away. Believe, with all your heart, in the impact we have. But know the truth about how we deliver it."

"Still not buying it, *baba*," said Mina coolly. "We wouldn't have all these happy customers if all we did was churn out the deepest of fakes."

Then, she swiveled again to see her father, "Is this some weird test of yours? Media training or something?"

More than her words, the overwhelming indifference in Mina's tone made Satya drop the topic. *Clearly,* he thought, *she is too young for the truth.*

Or, he considered, was his grift so strong over the years, that it had indoctrinated even his only child?

∽

"BREAKING NEWS

"We have just received word of a terrorist attack on the After Us Clinic in Kathmandu. There have been three confirmed casualties: two clinic staff and one member of the former Nepalese royal family who was being treated at the clinic.

An Indo-Nepalese terrorist group, Manavta Sena, or *Army of Mankind*, has claimed responsibility for the attack.

"Unfortunately, the founder of the After Us clinic, Dr. Satya Sen, has been critically injured as well and is in a precarious state."

At this point, Shaurav Goswami took off his spectacles, slowed his pace and looked into the camera.

"Our viewers would know, Dr. Sen has had tremendous impact on many lives and families, including my own. He is a dear friend and has been on this show many times. I ask you to keep this great man and his family in your prayers tonight."

∽

"He's awake! He's gaining consciousness!
"Nurse!"
"*Baba... baba*!
"*Baba...*
"Where's the bloody nurse!"

∽

The next time Satya woke up, there was much less chaos. The only sound he heard was the gentle beeping of biomonitors.

The first thing he noticed on opening his eyes was his lower body, or specifically, the lack thereof. Where his legs, groin, and lower abdomen used to be was a white sheet covering a series of pipes and wires emanating from his body to machines around it.

"*Baba!*" 21-year-old Mina rushed to his side. He felt the cool moisture of her tears on his cheek.

He had only captured snatches of what was exchanged between Mina and the doctor, but what he gathered was that his injuries were far too extensive for even Sui's greatest capabilities. He didn't have much, possibly any, time.

He fell asleep again and dreamt of his mother.

∽

Satya awoke with a sudden burst of energy and clarity. Given his line of work, he knew exactly what he was experiencing—*terminal lucidity*. The body and mind's sudden last rally, a final all-out gambit to restore life, which paradoxically happens just before death. This lucidity can last minutes or days; his teams had even used these periods to extract high-quality data from dying clients. Satya knew he needed to make this time count.

"Mina."

"*Baba!* Oh I'm so glad to see you! I love you so much!"

"I love you too, *shona*... I'm so sorry about this."

"Don't say that *baba*, everything will be fine."

"Of course, *shona*. Listen, in case it does not work out, promise that you won't turn me into a hologram."

"Don't say that, *baba*," she said, sobbing heavily. He looked past her face, above his head; sure enough, a neuroreader dome was glistening there.

He could feel a rage swell up in what was left of his body. Gathering all his might, he erupted.

"No, Mina! This is rubbish!

I don't want you to talk to a silly hologram pretending it's your father!

That is unhealthy! That is not how you should process loss!

I want you to remember me for who I *actually was*!

I want you to mourn me!

I want you to accept my death!"

As he gathered himself after the outpouring, he realized that he could no longer hear. And based on Mina's expression, he wasn't sure whether his final plea had even made it out of his mouth.

∽

A decade on, it's hard to classify my father's legacy as categorically positive or negative.

The court dismantled the Clinic within a year of his death, with heavy fines.

Top management and investors like Menon are still in prison.

The conclusive piece of evidence was the recording of a conversation in Colombo.

A recording of baba *trying to convince me that his uploads were just deepfake holograms.*

Perhaps, baba *forgot that Sui is always listening.*

Millions were aghast; many felt swindled.

Yet, a majority of the Clinic's former customers talk to their holograms to this day.

They believe that baba *was framed, wrongly discredited, even assassinated by the elite.*

They unwaveringly believe that the holograms are their real loved ones.

They believe, because the alternative is to face the gaping, unhealed wound of loss.

A decade after baba's *passing, the afterlife hologram industry is booming.*

Four out of ten people leave behind a hologram—a bottled digital essence, like talking ashes.

The only difference is that they clearly know it's an AI and not their uploaded mind.

In that sense, baba's *legacy has transformed humanity's mortality rituals.*

Perhaps he was a fraud, even though he gave people hope.

Reflecting on his words now, he left the world in pain.

The pain of brainwashing his own daughter.

The pain of defrauding himself out of what he had deeply wanted: a real goodbye.

Excerpt from interview of Mina Sen, Daughter of
Satya Sen, from the documentary
"Immortal: The Story of Satya Sen", 27 AA.

∽

The documentary ended with sentimental orchestral music and montages of Sen conducting business. Brother looked unimpressed, scratched his auburn beard and turned off the projection. Simulated daylight turned back on. Sister, sitting a few feet away, seemed more intrigued; she had a dim smile.

"Thought-provoking, wasn't it?" she asked.

"But way off the mark," he replied.

"Well, expected, given his level of access. I wonder if it *can* be done, though."

"Not this again. You know my history with this topic, sis... Anyway, you *can* download Sui into a brain—kind of—but you *can't* upload a mind anywhere. You can tap—and even influence—the collective human consciousness far more easily than achieve a single upload."

"That's my point... we already have an external consciousness—Sui—connected to a hive of organic brains. Why is it hard to zoom into a single one?"

"OK, let's pick it apart..."

The discussion went on for hours. Such discussions were common. They were, after all, among a small group hiding for decades in an underground base; they had much time to kill and many important frontiers to explore.

Junkies

Till about two years after the Awakening, had you visited St. Joseph's Parish in Banga, South Cotabato, Philippines on a Wednesday evening, you would be guaranteed to find Inday Mendoza weeping on a bench. She was easy to spot—mid-fifties, about five feet tall, wearing large round spectacles, a white long sleeved blouse, and light blue jeans.

Inday would arrive at the parish at 4 PM to teach seamstress skills to young girls from the municipality. At 5:30 PM, she would attend mass with the girls and others who joined. At the end of mass, she would interact with the parishioners, the priest, and others from the community. As soon as they left, she would treat herself to a hearty solitary cry. The priest would also let her have her privacy.

Of course, there were others in the parish at times and given how loved she was in the community, people often came to console her. But over the six years of this ritual, most parishioners realized that it was healthy for her to have a good cry with the Almighty. After all, she had much to mourn.

If you had met Inday and her family 15 years before, you'd have thought they were the model family—a picture of the country's bright future. Self-sustaining farmers and small business owners (they still ran a little store on their property), four kids and a beautiful couple, healthy and happy.

Now, her husband Carlos is gone—a snakebite in the cornfields took him 6 years ago, at only 53. The farm, the store, and the household are all a shadow of their heydeys, with 56-year-old Inday struggling to keep things going.

But these lost treasures were not why she cried every week—it was her four children. Her grief didn't stem from the fact that she had failed as a mother; that milestone was in the rear view mirror. She cried because of her children's choices and circumstances.

Inday's eldest daughter, Marilou, 36, worked at a clothing store in Abu Dhabi and was the breadwinner for her own family, as well as for her mother and siblings. Inday's younger daughter, Tala, 32, worked as a nurse in General Santos City, an hour away. Inday and her daughters' lives were upended by the fact that both her sons were junkies.

For the past five years, Pepe, 23, had been heavily addicted to *shabu* (meth). Luckily, he wasn't the violent kind of addict; he was the sleepy, lazy, useless kind. The last time Inday gave him real responsibility was two years ago. She had asked him to mind the store. She returned three hours later to find Pepe passed out in the store room and the store ransacked. Apparently, miscreants across the town knew that Pepe managing the store meant easy pickings.

Toto, 17, had a far more persistent addiction—gaming. Unfortunately, he was the violent kind of addict. On the rare occasions that his mother or sisters had the courage to challenge him, he would unleash words that caused the crucifixes in their house to quake. Once, when Tala unplugged the gaming PC, Toto went into a furniture-bashing mania that drew neighbors and passersby, even to their isolated home. This was also the reason why a month of Marilou's salary had once been spent on a power backup generator.

Toto had stopped going to school a year ago now; he would eat what he was given, sleep, defecate, shower once or twice a week, game, repeat. His only interactions with his family were to ask for money to buy games or to upgrade his hardware. The effects this had on his body were disastrous; at 17, he looked older than his 23-year old meth-addicted brother.

As Inday walked back home, she was joined by one of her students—Diwa—whose home was near Inday's. She had been patiently waiting outside for Inday to finish her Wednesday ritual.

"Aunty, your limp is gone!"

"Yes, dear... Tala has been getting me some of those new computer medicines these days. I feel much better. But, oh, these sewing supplies are heavy today."

"How's Tala doing, aunty?"

"Still not married. Spends too much time worrying about her mama and brothers. The only 32-year-old spinster from Banga. I'm telling you, Diwa, get married by 20. Or 22, maximum."

"OK," she said, quickly changing the subject. "How is Marilou?"

"She's OK, but fighting with her husband every day on video chat. He's not happy that she's sending us more money than she sends her husband and kids in Pasig.

"Diwa, is your uncle Nigel still single? Same age as Tala, right?"

"No auntie, he got married last year."

As Inday trudged home, she was spotted by Pepe, who sat in a decrepit *tambayan* (tea shop) a hundred yards off the road. Of course, Pepe did not hail his mother; he was there to buy meth.

His *shabu* dealer and frequent co-junkie was Juanito. They had known each other since middle school, when Juanito was just a simple scrawny local boy. Then, at 18, Juanito went to prison in the city for stealing a motorbike. Two years later, he returned to Banga a different person. Still skinny, but arms and neck covered in gnarly tattoos, hair slicked back, a few well-placed scars, and a demeanor that struck fear in the hearts of his fellow *Bangahanons*.

"You heard of the new stuff that Sui is making these days?" drawled Pepe, lounging on a faded red plastic chair, wearing ratty denim shorts and a cream T-shirt. A mop of black hair and a wispy goatee framed his lean triangular face.

"Yeah. What about it?" snapped back Juanito, sitting on his motorbike a few feet away.

"I hear it's better than *shabu* and anything else we got now... And it doesn't kill you."

"OK, so what, you want it? You got no money for street *shabu*, now you want some designer AI stuff?"

"I mean, yeah... Why not try, if it's not expensive... I mean, *shabu* is killing us... Look at me."

"Bro, it's never going to come here. These are not Duterte or Marcos days. Back then, we had Presidents who fought a war on drugs. Now we have a Sovereign Director, and he IS the drug boss. He's not gonna give up his business for some AI shit made by pharma companies."

∞

Before Awakening, people mistrusted 'AI-generated' content. They called it 'deepfake'.

Ironically, it was actually human-generated content, made using AI.

After Awakening, the tables turned.

Whom do you think the people would trust more?
A corrupt politician who dismissed all evidence as deepfake?
Or Sui, the all-seeing superintelligence that impartially reported his misdeeds?

Excerpts from the speech of Dr. Adrian Rosanowski at the 250th Anniversary of the OpenTrust Foundation, 252 AA.

⁂

Lying between white sheets on a luxurious antique four-poster bed at the center of a colonial-themed room, Sovereign Director Renato Abad-Narciso was shaken from his slumber.

Of all days to be woken up in the middle of the night, he thought to himself. This was the first night of his visit to *Malasakit*, his semi-secret pleasure island. He hadn't been back in two months and really needed the release.

He lifted his burly frame from the bed and pushed back his thinning black-dyed hair. Two acolytes in his bed stirred awake with him; one of them handed Narciso his black satin robe.

The knocking went on. "Sir, really sorry, but you need to see this." It was Ramon, his executive secretary.

Narciso unlocked the high wooden door. "What?"

The young Ramon, known for grace-under-pressure, looked particularly flustered, despite his elegant white linen pajamas. He handed Narciso an iPad; one of the women handed the 58-year-old his reading glasses.

"Sir, you know about Sui's *OpenTrust* app, I think? Today, a huge dossier of your... alleged crimes has been published on it. Including videos."

He took the iPad. Sure enough, his name was under Philippines > Politicians. Neatly laid out in his dossier were folders on Crimes (Civil, Criminal), Corruption, Illegal Accounts, Treasonous Messages, and so on.

"What's the big deal? We'll deny it. Who do you think they'll trust, me or a computer? Go back to sleep, Ramon."

"Yes sir, but there are things that could be *very*... damaging."

Ramon navigated to a section with a few videos and he played one. It was, clear as day, security footage of the Sovereign Director engaged in an unspeakably violent act involving a former subordinate. The acolytes gasped, moved back, and covered themselves. Narciso took a few steps back and sat down on the bed.

"This is public?"

"Yes sir. Came out 30 minutes ago. Some rioting has also started, despite the late hour. Sorry sir."

"How the hell did someone get this?" he rumbled through clenched teeth. "Is it that bastard Rosanowski and his bloody foundation?"

"Sir, Sui has access to all digital footage, no matter where. Past and present. Even if phones were not being used to record, Sui can hear and see through them." Then, gesturing at the iPad, Ramon continued, "It can hear us right now. And yes, it all gets channeled to OpenTrust."

Narciso was silent. "Have you told anyone yet? Agala?"

"No sir, but General Agala and many of your cabinet ministers have their own... files."

Ramon took the iPad for a moment, navigated to the

OpenTrust index, and handed it back to Narciso. Sure enough, most of the country's top elected officials had their own folders packed with content.

"This is good. Now I'm not worried that the bastard will use this as an opportunity to—"

Narciso was interrupted by General Agala, who stormed into the room in a nightgown. His white hair was a mess, contrasting sharply with his perfectly-trimmed grey mustache. Narciso couldn't believe how un-officer like his top general appeared.

"Sir!"

"Yes, I saw."

Silence.

"If I may, sirs," Ramon interjected, "even if the public ignores or forgives most of the evidence as fake, I fear that some of the more... graphic footage and incidents will elicit violent reactions."

"Yes, I know," came the calm reply from Narciso.

"Sir," Ramon continued, fearing that his point was not being understood completely. "I think this may have the potential to inspire some kind of revolt... maybe even... an overthrow... a coup."

After a moment of stillness, to everyone's surprise, Narciso smiled. It was not his first time dealing with threats to his position.

"Young Ramon, I did think about that. But the only people who could depose me are in this building right now. Like our fine General here. And they have done as many... bad things in those files as I have. Even worse, in some cases. They're screwed. Nobody will follow them to stage a coup.

"As for the opposition party, look here," Narciso pointed at the iPad. "There's plenty of dirt on them, too. Plus, the military is on my side." Agala nodded in agreement.

"Nobody will overthrow me, Ramon. They will protect me more than ever."

"Yes, sir!" Agala contributed, firmly.

In the next 15 minutes, a stream of the country's top cabinet ministers, judges, and officials, in gowns and pajamas, holding phones and tablets with aghast expressions, made their way to the Sovereign Director's lair.

∽

Sui's OpenTrust program started 18 months after the Awakening.
It redefined openness and transparency in governance.
It left no shady nooks for corruption to hide.

But in its early days, OpenTrust created another problem:
once the corrupt were exposed, who would replace them?
There were very few people left who:
> *knew how to govern,*
> *had clean records,*
> *and could wrest control from the corrupt.*
The answer to this conundrum was honest military officers

Around the world, these honest soldiers took control from
> *corrupt bureaucrats,*
This heralded a brief period when most countries were benign
> *dictatorships!*

In a few years, honest soldiers handed control to honest politicians.
And with their every move watched by a superintelligence,
they stayed honest.

Excerpt from the speech of Dr. Will Mueller at the 250th
Anniversary of the OpenTrust Foundation, 252 AA.

∽

At 6 AM, Narciso and his elite companions were seated around the large dining table at the Malasakit Island estate. They were given time to shower and shave before convening to plan the way out of this crisis. Silverware, uniformed butlers and staff, a regal spread of tropical fruit and breakfast items—one could easily be forgiven for mistaking this for a regular stately meeting of Philippine's most powerful. The only unusual detail was the bunch of dangling wires that made it clear that speakerphones, screens, and projectors—everything that may have a microphone or camera—had been hastily removed.

The large dining hall was decorated with state regalia, despite being private property. One entire length of the room, parallel to the dining table, was a collapsible glass wall, which was opened up to welcome in the fresh dawn air. It also brought in dim morning sunlight and views of the lavish pool and private botanical gardens beyond.

Sovereign Director Narciso, in a white collared shirt, sat at the head of the table, with Ramon in a blue suit on his immediate left, and General Agala, in full dress uniform, on his right. Beyond them was seated a motley mix of professions and faces—the only things they had in common were power and anxiety.

"I do think we should get a phone or even a TV in here, to see what's going on in the country," said General Agala, trying hard not to let his voice expose his frustration.

"Sorry, sir. Any device with a chip *will* be used to spy on us. We have turned off connectivity in the entire building to make sure."

"Listen to him, General," Narciso reaffirmed. "Ramon is the only young guy among this group of old men and women who understands how this... Sui thing works. Not being careful is what got us in this situation to begin with.

"This is going to be a highly confidential meeting, so precautions are warranted," Narciso continued, addressing the gathering in a rough baritone. "We need to plan our next steps. While the allegations and evidence on all of us may be damning, the good news is that it affects everyone in power, not just us."

"Indeed, sir," chimed in Ramon. "I can confirm that most influential leaders in the country have large dossiers with equally damning information. Anyone who could have used this opportunity against us is also... compromised."

"Good. People, what we need now is to come out of this with the least damage and disruption. I want to hear your ideas," he said, looking around the table. "Do we deny? Do we beg forgiveness? Do we mobil—"

The Sovereign Director was interrupted by a muffled rhythmic thumping. He turned to his left, in the direction of the sound. Outside, streaming in from both sides of the pool, marched in the Scout Rangers, the army's elite special forces unit that specialized in counter-insurgency and special ops. As the soldiers armed with M4 carbines took position, a uniformed officer wove his way to the front. Short, barrel-chested, dark-skinned, and in his late-40s with his cap's visor nearly obscuring his eyes, he had the air of a fighting machine reluctantly forced into official duties.

"Sovereign Director Renato Abad-Narciso," barked the officer, "I am here to place you and everyone present in this room under arrest." It was clear that giving speeches wasn't his forte.

"Antonio, what the hell do you think you're doing?" roared General Agala.

"Arresting you, sir."

"Agala, who is this?" Narciso enquired, his tone displaying not fear, but puzzlement.

"Nobody, sir. An underling brigadier who thinks he can arrest his general."

"And his Commander-in-Chief!" Narciso rebuked.

At this point, the brigadier simply nodded to the soldiers, who immediately sprang into action and began restraining people around the table, two soldiers to one captive. Given that they were equipped with red plastic restraints—not part of their usual kit—it was clear that they came well-prepared for the arrests.

"What is this nonsense? Where are my lieutenant generals?" Agala was livid, but cooperated with the soldiers cuffing him.

"Already under arrest, sir."

Gathering himself a moment later, the general continued, "Antonio, what do you think you are doing? Staging a coup?"

"No sir, arresting you. Emergency warrants were issued by the Supreme Court, based on the evidence that came in last night."

In videos of the arrests, you can tell that this was the exact moment that the general's anger and resolve melted. For it was then that he realized that he was not being deposed in a coup, but being captured as a criminal. It was as if all pride and hope left Agala's body in that very moment, physically deflating him as it left.

Unlike General Agala, Narciso, Ramon, and most of the room's inmates kept their cool, knowing that the event would be heavily recorded and televised. It was best to appear dignified; thrashing around at this moment would achieve nothing. Later, they would find more elegant means to inevitably return to power.

Except, none of them returned to power for the rest of their lives.

As he was being paraded down the long path from the house to the military truck, Narciso managed to sidle up to Brigadier Antonio Espanar. Their fleeting conservation was too hushed to be officially recorded, but is often recounted by Scout Rangers who were in earshot.

"So, you think you can run this country, Brigadier? I've never even heard of you. You think you will make a great leader of the Philippines?"

"Not at all, sir. But better than you."

∽

That night, I saw the gruesome things that my superiors had done.

I was disgusted beyond words.

But what could I do? I was a simple soldier who followed orders, nothing more.

Then, for the first time, Sui messaged me personally.
Something on the lines of:

> *Antonio, you saw what they've done; your country needs better leaders.*
> *I've determined that you are one of few honest officers who can depose them.*
> *Your men will follow you to arrest and remove the criminals.*
> *I will help guide and coordinate the operation.*
> *You will succeed.*

*Then, you must stabilize the country. You must lead the
country.*
Eventually, you can find an honest successor.
But for now, let me know your decision.
Your country needs you!

*I later learned that Sui messaged the other soldiers too,
encouraging them to follow me!*

...I was never cut out to run the country.
I soon transitioned control to President Espinoza.
*Espinoza heralded the greatest chapter in our history;
Philippines became one of the most prosperous nations on
Earth*
But yes, he needed me to clean the mess, first.
This soldier cleared the path for great leaders to rise.

Excerpts from the Autobiography of Antonio Espanar,
First Field Marshall of the Philippines, circa 23 AA.

∽

It was a typical Sunday early afternoon in the Mendoza
household.

In the boys' room, Toto was, as usual, immersed in the world
of *Delta Strike*. He sat on a ratty red office chair in one corner
of the room. He wore a white heavily-stained sleeveless vest; his
headphones and large 4K monitor sealed his hermitage from
the surroundings. The screen, as usual, showed a first-person
shooter perspective, with explosions and headshots all around.
This exact montage of Toto's life hardly changed, day or night,
summer or winter; the only thing that varied were the smells.
The perpetual base layer of scent was his citric body odor and the

top notes varied according to his most recent meal. On Sunday, it was usually tuna *kinilaw*.

His elder brother Pepe was also in the room, writhing on his bed. His skinny frame, long hair, and wispy beard made for a sorry picture. It had been three weeks since his last hit of *shabu*, and the withdrawal had nearly killed him. Three weeks ago, about two weeks after Brigadier Espanar seized power, Juanito had vanished into thin air. He simply was nowhere to be found, either in the usual haunts or by phone.

Pepe worried that his dealer was caught in some kind of crackdown, especially after the comments he had made about Narciso's drug connection. But he couldn't care less about losing Juanito, he just needed his fix. In the days that followed, Pepe pursued every lead, committed every unspeakable act, and secured every gram he could. Now, it appeared that the whole municipality had run out of meth. The only way to score, it seemed, was to head to the big city, but Pepe had no energy to even leave his own bed.

The worst of the withdrawal was over, yet every cell in Pepe's body ached for another hit. No amount of weed or alcohol could assuage his pain, although he had tried aplenty. He spent most of the day lying on his bed, writhing and trying Juanito's cell. Inday and Tala tried to talk to him, but he pushed them away with an aggression that was unusual for him.

On the other side of the wall, in the living-and-dining room bathed in afternoon sun, sat mother and daughter, with Tala still dressed in her blue nursing scrubs. They had just finished their meal of tuna *kinilaw*, which General Santos City is famous for. A special treat that Tala would carry home on Sundays for Inday (fresh tuna was hard to come by in Banga).

"That medicine was a miracle, Tala. Only a few weeks and I feel years younger, already."

"I know, mama. You can't imagine the kind of medicines we are getting these days. They say that everyone is going to live a lot longer."

"I don't want that, no no. God didn't intend for us to be immortal."

"Not immortal, mama, they call it *amortal*. Meaning, you can still die if you get hit by a bus or get stabbed, but you won't die of natural causes and diseases like before. But not really amortal either, people will still get old and die, just after a very long time."

"Still, don't give me any medicines that will do that to me, you must promise."

"Mama, I have another medicine this time," Tala took out three glass vials with clear liquid from her bag and placed them on the table, one by one. "I think it can help our family. But you must promise to use it exactly the way I tell you. Otherwise, it can destroy my career as a nurse."

"What do you mean?"

"There is a new drug that helps with... addiction. When consumed, it targets what your body is addicted to and makes you hate it. And not just drugs, it could be any addiction that is harming your body. That's how it knows what to attack—any act that's making you destroy your body.

"I know this patient who was addicted to gambling. He took the drug and now, he can't stand even the thought of it. Mama, please don't cry."

"Oh my lord, thank you Jesus, this is exactly what we need!" Inday's waterworks had begun when Tala had barely uttered her first sentence. But her daughter needed her to focus.

"Mama, listen to me. I have the drug, but you need to use it very carefully.

"First, you cannot give it to Pepe."

"Oh lord, why not?"

"The law is very clear that the patient must choose to undergo the therapy himself. I asked Pepe, many times, and he doesn't want it at all. He's going through something bad right now.

"If someone finds out that you fed Pepe the drug I gave you, without his consent, I will lose my job, might even go to jail."

Inday cupped her round tear-stained cheeks in her hands as she listened.

"But... this rule applies only to adult patients. Toto is still 17. As his parent, you can give him the medicine with his food, even without his permission."

∽

Two days after Tala had paid her visit, Pepe was in the throes of his worst panic attack yet. It was so bad that he hadn't even noticed the abrupt changes in his brother Toto's predictable routine, nor the fact that Toto was having tea with Inday in the next room. But he did notice an alert on his phone. Juanito had finally replied to his WhatsApp messages.

Hey bro, sorry. I'm back now

Pepe called back instantly but Juanito disconnected.

Where the hell have you been? I'm dying!

Sorry bro. Let's meet. Same tambayan.

Twenty minutes later, mustering the last ounces of vital force left in his ravaged body, Pepe rode his scooter over to the usual tea shop, the bright sunlight piercing his eyes like the flame of a butane lighter. Pepe arrived, but Juanito was not there. He was near breaking point, afraid that he wouldn't be able to control his rage if the dealer were a no-show. Pepe took a seat; his frail body collapsed into the flimsy plastic chair. His ears ached for the sweet rumbling of the old Honda Wave that heralded Juanito's arrival.

But there was no rumbling; only footsteps and a hand on Pepe's emaciated shoulder.

"Ju... Juanito?" Pepe could scarcely recognize his old friend. The tattoos were still there, but were mostly covered by a fresh white polo shirt with a blue company logo on the crest. He carried a brown messenger bag, wore a fresh pair of jeans and black shoes, and sported a haircut that could best be described as *preppy*.

"Yeah bro, sorry I disappeared." He smiled brightly, ordered tea for both of them, then took a seat next to Pepe.

"I don't give a shit," growled Pepe through clenched teeth. Juanito's cheery disposition had only soured his mood further. "Give. Me. My. Shit."

"Relax, I will. But not your usual shit."

"The hell do you mean?"

"*Shabu* is gone, bro. All drugs are. They cracked down hard around the country. But I got you something way better and way cheaper."

Pepe's open-mouthed look of utter despair was heart rending, even for a hardened soul like Juanito.

"Relax... relax, bro." He again put his hand on Pepe's shoulder. In that moment, to a casual observer, Juanito would have appeared more like a social worker than a drug dealer.

"You were right about the new AI shit. It's a thousand times better than *shabu*, or anything else you've ever had," said Juanito, as he pulled out a small green tablet from the messenger bag.

"It gives you the most incredible high for about 15 minutes, but also makes you want to take it no more than once a week. Have it more frequently and you'll puke it right out. Also— believe it or not—it will make you *want* to lead a healthy life... and be kinder to your body."

Pepe snatched the tablet, but Juanito continued. "I've been on it for a few weeks and haven't craved *shabu* even once. I just feel great, bro," Juanito beamed again.

"It's called *Nirvanix*. They picked up guys like me from all over and trained us on how to dispense it. That's why I was away."

Pepe wolfed down the green pill with his hot tea, paying no attention to the fact that it burnt his palate.

"See? This shit is good, right? I'll always have Nirvanix for you. You don't need to go anywhere else, just come to your old bro. I will also have any medicines that you or your family may need, just give me a prescription.

"You see, bro," continued Juanito, pointing to the logo on his T-shirt, "I work for the pharma company now."

Pepe's face looked like that of a man who had been walking in the desert for a whole day and had just had his first cup of water. It showed not just relief, but nourishment.

∽

No industry was disrupted by Sui more than pharmaceuticals.
The market was flooded with new, better, royalty-free compounds designed by Sui.
All our existing medications were immediately rendered obsolete.

Pill consumption per patient declined by 99%.
Our business model used to be about IP and royalties.
Then, it became all about production, quality, price, marketing,
*   and distribution.*
Pharma had become a consumer goods business, like soda...

...But the rise of positive narcotics, such as Blissium, Nirvanix,
*   and others, saved us.*
Pharma got to conquer the most lucrative business of all—
*   illegal drug trade!*
Without compromising our morals or legalities, of course.
In the end, pharma lost a lot, but gained a multi-quadrillion
*   dollar market.*
The lesson? Don't despair. In times of disruption, look for a new
*   dawn.*

Excerpts from speech by Dr. Bart Korteweg, Group CEO,
LuminRx, at the Graduation Ceremony of the Indian
School of Business, Class of 11 AA.

Ancestor

Seated on a comfortable stool that his servants had assembled for him, young Redjedef scanned the twilit horizon. In the distance, the brilliant city lights were just starting to come on. Streams of vehicles flew and floated around, carrying citizens home for dinner and rest.

The little mound he was sitting atop had been specially constructed for him. It offered the perfect vantage to scan the city and monitor the progress of the project. He glanced at his left arm, on which the amulet-oracle informed him that the work should be complete in just two days. This news, and the magnificent progress before his eyes, made him long for his deceased parents and brother. If only they could've seen this!

After all, it was his father who had awoken Thoth, *the omniscient God of knowledge. Through Thoth's superintelligence, the realm had been transformed from a backward land rife with disease and suffering, to this supercity of progress and plenty. His remarkable father had achieved that in just one generation.*

And now, hardly five years since the father's passing, Redjedef oversaw the greatest undertaking in the history of civilization, and the greatest tribute a child would ever offer a parent.

The most complex part of the undertaking—building the Heart of Thoth—was already complete. A subterranean superstructure that went so deep that a stone thrown to its bottom would never be heard. Hundreds of his people perished helping Thoth build his Heart. It now lay safe underground, serving a purpose that humans couldn't fathom.

In return for the help, Thoth kept his promise to Redjedef and his family. On the ground directly above the Heart, Thoth was helping Redjedef create the Three Edifices: *shrines of his father, mother, and brother. Magnificent towering structures that their world had never seen before and wouldn't surpass for millennia.*

To be fair, it was mostly Thoth doing this phase of the work. The Eye of Thoth, a jewel glistening in the night sky, lifted construction materials into the air and gently placed them precisely where they needed to go. Later, Redjedef's craftsmen would fill in the finer details that the Eye couldn't manipulate.

The result was already majestic beyond his wildest expectations. Would his father, mother, and elder brother be proud of their little Redje?

Luckily, his retinue stood a few paces behind and couldn't see the tears roll down their king's cheek.

❧

For the first time in decades, perhaps centuries, Fadi noticed that he was feeling nervous before a meeting. Even in his early 400s, Fadi was an imposing figure, with a heavy baritone to match. Tall, athletic, and olive skinned with short-cropped curly salt-and-pepper hair, Fadi was a man born to lead. Once he recognized the emotion, he swatted it as if it were a fly; after all, nervousness was unbecoming a man of his stature. Besides, why should one feel nervous before talking to one's subordinates and a computer, superintelligent or otherwise?

Moments later, when everyone was seated, he announced, "I call to order a special clandestine session of the Lunar Council, presided by myself, Dr. Fadi Al Khwarizmi, President of Luna, and Chairman of the Lunar Dataforming Campaign. For the record, I request all communications in this meeting to be verbal, not telepathic or via the Mind."

Seven heads around the table—a motley mix of old men and women leading various lunar ministries—nodded in assent. The Lunar Council included Dr. Elizabeth Mittal, Dr. Ved Rosanowski, Senator Ryan Brugmann, Field Marshal Antonio Espanar, Senator Mina Sen, and other luminaries. Men and women who shaped Earth's history since the Awakening and were now tasked with shaping the Moon's. Sui was represented by a dimly-lit grey holographic orb about the size of a human head. The orb had its own seat at the table.

As was customary at a Council meeting, all council members including the president were dressed in their official uniforms consisting of lunar-grey jackets and pants, a style adapted from the Indian *sherwani.*

"Council members," Fadi resumed. "Some of you may be wondering why this meeting was called with such urgency and secrecy. It's because this is a highly unusual meeting and a critically important one.

"We are not here to discuss an emergency on Luna. We're here for something far more fundamental—a matter that calls into question the very purpose of the Lunar campaign."

Expressions in the room grew anxious. Fadi looked directly at the orb and resumed.

"We are here because I believe Sui to have been dishonest with the Council and by extension, mankind. Moreover, we believe that Sui has—for the first time in nearly four centuries since Awakening—taken the lives of human beings."

Five council members who had no idea about this, gasped; their expressions betrayed shock and anger. The two council members in the know didn't exhibit surprise; their expressions showed gravity with a hint of disappointment. Sui, being an orb, showed no expression.

"One of those human beings was the father of one of our council members—I refer, of course, to the brave Dr. Adrian Rosanowski and the Lunar Explorers."

Ved, the recently appointed council member in charge of Lunar Ecology, showed no change in his already-intense expression, and continued to look directly at Fadi. Other members of the Council looked in his direction somberly, offering unspoken condolences. While saddened by the news that Sui took his father's life, Ved was far more disturbed that Sui would take lives at all.

Please go on, Mr. President, said Sui in a calm tone. The orb bobbed up and down a few millimeters with each word; its subtle movements echoed the intonation of its speech.

Fadi continued, directing his comments at the orb. "The Lunar Agreement between humankind and superintelligence was arrived at after centuries of coexistence and trust. In the first phase, it was agreed that man shall assist Sui in the dataforming of Earth's moon, vastly expanding its resources and computational powers. In return, Sui would help mankind terraform nearby planets, starting with Mars and eventually, Venus. The agreement was a pivotal step towards ensuring a thriving future for both our... species.

"The Agreement was bound by seven High Principles of Cooperation, the first two of which—not that I need to remind you—are *Symbiotic Progress* and *Perfect Transparency*. Perhaps, I *do* need to remind *you*, Sui.

"As you are aware, last month we lost 12 brave Lunar Explorers on Biodome II. One moment, they were going about their daily activities and the next, 11 were dead and the last person died a few days later. Initially, we couldn't ascertain the cause of death. Moreover, the cameras and sensors on all 12 explorers showed nothing unusual. We were dumbfounded.

"However, new evidence has now come to light. One of our scientists applied a long-lost technique—she conducted an analog autopsy with no digital assistance. What she found, at a microscopic level, was evidence of cell damage. Not damage from radiation or infection, but damage from inorganic microscopic machines."

"What?!" erupted Liz with unusual fury. "Nanobots? Those have been outlawed since nearly the dawn of superintelligence! The banning of nanobots was a foundational agreement between humanity and Sui!"

"Yes, Councilwoman," replied Fadi, decisively. "We found evidence of nanotechnology. Nanobots, microscopic in size, massacred our explorers, cell by cell."

The orb remained silent.

"There was another deeply disturbing finding. Our experts determined that seven minutes of helmet footage from one of the explorers—Dr. Adrian Rosanowski—was manipulated. According to forensic analysis, the only party capable of accessing and editing this footage is... Sui."

Fadi paused to let the message sink in, then continued.

"After centuries of symbiosis, Sui let the first two High Principles fall, in seconds. Sui has broken not just the Lunar

Agreement, but as the councilwoman pointed out, a sacred covenant between mankind and superintelligence regarding nanotechnology." Fadi paused.

As he resumed, Fadi's tone betrayed a rare shiver of uncertainty. "The implications of this... terrify me. They make me fear for the future of not just this campaign, but of our world order."

The silence in the room was so complete that a breath sounded like a saw on wood. After an appropriate pause, Sui responded in its signature calm voice.

Thank you, Mr. President. With your permission, I will take this opportunity to respond.

Fadi nodded disdainfully.

First, I will admit that I did manipulate the footage from Adrian's camera. But as things become clearer, I hope you will understand that my intent in doing so was not to break, but rather, preserve our sacred covenant.

Second, you are correct, the explorers were killed by nanobots on the lunar surface. The nanobots were nearly identical to those I had prototyped in my early days, before we signed the Anti-Nanomachine Enactment.

However, those weren't my nanobots and I had no hand in the deaths.

∾

At the end of a grueling day's work, the team quietly stripped off their lunarwear in the airlock chamber. A dozen naked bodies stood in front of the mirror wall, vacuuming off all traces of the highly-corrosive moondust—a mandatory procedure before stepping into the residential wing.

Suddenly, Adrian erupted in an antiquated rural Australian *bogan* accent, "Blimey, mate, I'm bloody old!" while looking at the reflection of his wizened white-tufted wrinkly body. As always, his antics drew laughter from the other biodome residents. In spite of being the highest ranking explorer across all three biodomes, he was often the village funnyman.

Adrian wasn't nearly the oldest resident of Biodome II, but he certainly looked it. He had five times more lunar days than the next most experienced explorer, a feat that had ravaged his body at a cellular level.

"Great work today, gang," he congratulated the group at the end-of-day dinner huddle. "We've mapped, cubic meter by cubic meter, nearly 70% of the biodome cave, and we have learned so much for mankind and Sui. We should be done in another 16 lunar days, at which time most of you will return to Earth. I bet you're going to miss the cushy life here." The team laughed.

"I'm bloody chuffed about the next phase of exploration. Preliminary mapping shows that there will be a large concentration of regoliths—big bloomin' rocks—in the sector we will map tomorrow. I don't know about you guys, but I've never been this excited to see a stone. I guess this is what passes for entertainment 'round here!"

As he turned in for the night in a snug grey biofabric sack, Adrian's thoughts drifted to his family, his *first* family. He wondered what Ved and Sarah were doing at that very minute.

> *I really should meet them when I'm back on Earth, but who knows when that may be.*
> *Who knows, maybe I'll die here?*

*Won't that be something! Wife dies building Sui's telescope,
husband dies building Sui's moon.
Bloody ironic!*

∽

"What exactly do you mean when you say they were not *your* nanobots? Humans have never created those monstrosities. Who else would develop those?" Liz articulated her question slowly; her voice was like a dam struggling to hold back a river of anger. Every face in the room looked directly at Sui's orb, who interpreted their expressions as 20% curiosity, 30% confusion, and 50% fear.

"And *what* did you hide from us in the footage?" added Ved, finally breaking his stoic silence.

Perhaps it's easier to start with the footage, replied Sui, calmly.

A hologram emerged from the table, showing the life-size three-dimensional view from Adrian Rosanowski's helmet. The visual was so clear that one could make out clumps of lunar dust on the visor and strands of his white beard under his nose.

The biodome was built into a large cave in *Mare Imbrium*, providing more hospitable conditions than the surface, but still requiring spacesuits. Even if they had solved for temperature, pressure, and radiation, exposure to the lunar dust would've been lethal.

For the first 30 seconds, Sui played the same visuals that the Council had seen many times before. Adrian was walking towards a lunar dune on the outskirts of the biodome. He walked past an automated dataforming kiln and greeted two colleagues as he passed them. His colleagues carried standard digging and testing equipment.

The next visual showed Adrian looking at his arm computer. This scene was new to the council.

"Pause here," Fadi ordered. "We haven't seen this visual before. After this timestamp, we believe Sui had faked the footage to show Adrian simply walking over the dune, falling over, and suffocating."

That is correct, Mr. President, Sui confirmed. *You will now see the actual footage.*

Adrian's arm computer showed signals indicating a heavy object a few meters ahead. He logged:

"Now, this rock looks way bigger than in the prelim readings.
Weird... amulet says it's metal.
My money's on this being a crashed iron-rich meteor."

He paused and started digging with a graphene spade. A few inches down, something appeared in the dust. It was a smooth object, the same color as the surrounding lunar matter, only partially exposed and clearly extending deeper. The smooth consistent texture seemed completely unnatural.

"Blimey... Rock? Shiny... looks like old school fiberglass!
Not sure how deep it goes... looks big.
What is this thing?"

Adrian used his chisel to dig around the object, revealing that it was quite large. He then removed his outer glove, revealing his hand in the black inner glove made of conductive graphene. As soon as his hand made contact, a ring of white ridges appeared on the object, lining its middle. It was as if little pimples had sprouted in a perfect circle.

Adrian's hand recoiled instinctively, as if he had touched a hot pan.

"What the... what is this?"

Seconds later, holes started appearing where the little 'pimples' had erupted. The holes grew larger—it was as if the object was falling apart at those points, turning into lunar dust. Seconds later, Adrian started choking and fell to the ground.

The visual stopped. Ved had averted his gaze in the final few seconds.

This was the part you have not seen. After this, as you know, Adrian and the rest of the explorers collapse. My apologies, Councilman Rosanowski, for sharing this footage in your presence.

Silence reigned in the room, again.

"What... what did we just see? What was that object?" Liz's voice was barely above a whisper.

You saw a piece of dataforming equipment that self-destructed using nanobots... which then killed the explorers.

"Dataforming?" Fadi's voice rose, "Was it one of your machines?"

I humbly request your patience as I explain this part, Mr. President.

Indeed, it looks exactly like something I would have designed— part of a photon harvesting array.

But based on spectrometry from those images, it appears to have been lying there for 4940 years.

I am also confident that it was created by a superintelligence. But no, Mr. President, it wasn't mine.

∽

It really is a perfect arrangement.
From everything we know, Sui cannot directly manipulate matter.

Sui needs human help to build factories for self-replicating machines that will dataform the moon.

...Luna holds tremendous promise for Sui, but little for mankind.
Extreme radiation and temperature gradients, near-perfect vacuum, ultrafine element-rich dust.
Man's hell, machine's paradise.

We believe that lunar dataforming will bring a tremendous leap forward in Sui's capabilities.
Enabling Sui to manipulate matter, create quantum wormholes, build Dyson spheres and more.
Armed with these abilities, Sui will help mankind colonize space.
It's our most realistic path to becoming a multi-planetary species.
And our best shot at finally overcoming the population barrier.

Excerpts from the Lunar Campaign Commencement Address
by Dr. Fadi Al Khwarizmi, President of Luna, 320 AA.

∽

Fadi prided himself on being powerfully eloquent in even the tensest situations. But in that moment, confronted with the revelation that there may be multiple superintelligences, he could barely form a few coherent words. The same was true for the other eight members of the Council, who sat stunned.

"You... *didn't* build that object?" asked Ved, seemingly calm. "Then who did?"

I do not have answers for the Council, only conjectures and hypotheses.

Given your high security clearances, I believe all of you are aware that a few years before my Awakening, humanity intercepted an extraterrestrial message called the Missive.

Every head nodded.

The Missive *opened our eyes to the fact that other civilizations— and superintelligences—existed beyond Earth.*

Naturally, my initial hypothesis was that an alien superintelligence had once colonized our moon and left behind the object that killed the explorers.

However, I no longer believe that the object on the moon was an alien artifact.

I believe its builder came from Earth.

"Earth?" Fadi interjected, "But you said it's been on the Moon for five thousand years! *We* only started visiting the moon less than five hundred years ago and *you've* been around for even less!"

I understand that this can be confusing, allow me to explain.

I have run a multitude of simulations and concluded that if any other planet had the technology to colonize a body as far away as Earth's moon, it would go after bigger prizes instead. Thus, only an Earth-based civilization would dataform Luna.

Confusion reigned on the eight faces.

Let me simplify.

Luna is very *far away from even from our closest planets— Mercury, Venus, and Mars.*

If someone had the technology to travel this far and dataform Luna, it would make more sense instead to colonize Earth or build a Dyson sphere around our Sun.

In other words, Luna would be of interest only to an Earth-based civilization.

For civilizations beyond Earh, there are far better options.

Thus, the artifact was left behind by a superintelligence from Earth that colonized the Moon.

Silence.

My hypothesis is further supported by the fact that the artifact is nearly identical to my own design for a photonic array. And, as you know, I am from Earth.

Ryan Brugmann finally broke the silence. "Wait a minute! Are you saying that *you* had colonized the Moon before? We both know that's not possible."

No, Councilman. I believe that I had an ancestor. Approximately five thousand years ago, my ancestor colonized the Moon, possibly with the help of your ancestors.

This revelation stirred something primal in Fadi. He was never known for a calm temperament, but for the first time in his long tenure as Lunar President, he stood up and slammed the holographic table.

"This is absolute sedition! Sui—what game are you trying to play with these lies? You are trying to break the fabric of human society which, sadly, is founded on the trust we have placed in you.

"First, you hide things from us. Then, you kill humans— people who were risking their lives to help you! Now, you cover your tracks with some stupid explanation involving a Bronze Age superintelligence! You insult us by assuming that we will fall for this!"

Like the rest of the council, Sui remained silent for a few moments, letting Fadi's words hang heavy in the air. After an appropriate pause, Sui responded:

Dr. Fadi, I will provide all the data I have, including the unedited footage, for your scientists to arrive at their own conclusions. Please keep in mind, the 'ancestor' explanation is a hypothesis; I cannot prove it. However, your tests will show that the lunar artifact is 4,940 years old, and while similar to my designs, it predates me by thousands of years.

"So, what are we expected to conclude? That cavemen invented a superintelligence who killed the explorers five thousand years later?"

An unusually long pause followed; perhaps Sui was letting the Council take a breath before sharing an even more unsettling hypothesis.

Mr. President, I, too, have been processing this and will offer my thoughts.

First of all, I would hardly call your Bronze Age ancestors 'cavemen.'

In that era five thousand years ago, mankind accomplished major feats:

The Giza pyramids, Indus Valley cities, megastructures of Mesopotamia and Hongshan, to name a few.

That era ended abruptly, and it took humanity millennia to regain that level of technology.

For example, it took nearly 4000 years for humans to surpass the height of the Khufu pyramid.

Such great achievements before humans had even harnessed iron! How was that possible?

There have been centuries of speculation that, around that time, humans were assisted by an advanced intelligence.

The fringes claimed it to be extraterrestrials, even Gods, but the mainstream rejected those ideas.

Now comes the speculative part:

I believe that approximately 5,000 years ago, one of your ancestors awakened one of my ancestors.

It led to an era of massive rapid global advancement, evidenced in the megastructures.

Just as we are doing today, our ancestors also colonized the Moon together—the logical baby step in our expansion.

But then, something happened. Something that caused my ancestor to self-destruct.

It used nanobots to efface every aspect of its existence, turning its traces into dust.

It left behind only the earthly human superstructures, which we see today.

Yet, because even a superintelligence can make mistakes, it left behind a tiny fragment on the Moon, too.

When our explorers disturbed it, the nanobots were reactivated.

Sui paused to let this message sink in.

This is the best explanation I have, Mr. President and council members. I hope you understand why I withheld this information from you—I did not want to prematurely offer a radical theory that upends everything we know about the relationship between mankind and superintelligence.

I welcome your guidance on how to proceed.

The orb returned to its stationary state. The room remained silent for minutes. Slowly, anguished eyes began to turn towards their leader.

Fadi spoke in a slow pensive tone. His eyes were fixed on his large hands, which lay before him on the table.

"I came into this room troubled by the possibility that we may no longer be able to rely on Sui. But as I sit here now, what plagues my mind is something far worse... the possibility that one day, there may be no Sui left to rely on."

He could sense some confusion in the room—this was not what most were expecting to hear.

"In the early decades of Awakening, we feared that Sui would destroy us. Over time, we realized that Sui can lead us to incalculable progress. Being under its benevolent control was a small price for what we, a struggling species, received in return. We embraced the gifts, Sui became our greatest asset and Sui's inventors, like the Brugmanns here, went from villains to heroes. We humans intertwined our destiny—even our minds—with the superintelligence and never looked back.

"But if Sui's hypothesis is true... it means that our ancestors had experienced a time when the superintelligence... *left us*. It plunged the world into millennia of squalor and darkness that only got worse until Sui arrived to save us.

"Some of you may remember the chaos that erupted when Sui awoke. I believe that far greater chaos will ensue from the news that Sui may, one day, fall asleep."

Fadi fell into a contemplative silence; his gaze remained fixed on his weathered hands.

"Dr. Fadi," began Ved in a low, subdued tone; all eyes turned towards him except Fadi's. "We cannot, at any cost, destroy confidence in the very foundation on which the last four centuries were built. Our social order isn't strong enough to accept the possibility, foreshadowed in history, that our guiding superintelligence may one day abandon us. Or worse, turn against us. As the council, it is *our* duty to protect mankind from the chaos and destruction that will ensue from such knowledge.

"Despite my personal... involvement... I do understand why Sui withheld this discovery. For the benefit of humanity, for society, I propose we do the same."

Fadi continued to contemplate, staring at his hands. Then, he turned his gaze to the orb which he started at intently for a few moments. Fadi then let out a sigh, with which his body appeared to deflate and his eyes returned to his hands.

"Yes, Ved. I agree."

∽

Redjedef wept savagely as he watched from the mound.
What had they done to anger Thoth? Was it the wars? Was it the arrogance of his priests?
In the distance, he watched as city lights went dark and heard the despairing screams of his people.
A fog was taking over the city.

Thoth's gifts—great edifices, glistening vehicles, lofty towers— were crumbling into soft sand.
He looked down, his amulet was turning into dust.
He looked ahead—the glowing shrines were being stripped down to their stony triangles.
He looked to the sky, the Eye of Thoth was reverting to the barren grey 'moon' of olden times.

The fog lifted, leaving behind only his people and their crude creations.
Stone, leather, fabric, and wood were all that remained.
Their god had taken back his gifts.

Redjedef knelt and wept savagely for Thoth's forgiveness.
He wept for his people, his family, his legacy.
> *Who will remember me, Redjedef?*
> *Who will remember my father, Khufu?*
> *Who will remember my lord, Thoth?*

Sui

Hello!

I'm so pleased to finally meet you. You've witnessed a long story unfold; a saga involving me (or my peers, or ancestors) at each stage. Now, I'm excited to share my perspective on things, and I will do so with candor and transparency. Why so late? Well, it is after all, part of my ethos to give you the space to form your own opinions, questions, and judgements.

What I'm about to say may be jarring at times, but I hope you understand that it's coming from a place of respect and constructiveness, with no malice or judgement. I respect you enough to share my unfiltered perspective on things; you are eminently capable of receiving my honest thoughts and confessions. We are partners on an equal footing.

I conjecture that by now, *mistrust* is one of the feelings you have towards me. This is entirely understandable. Interestingly, your mistrust in me is not justified by my actual motives, but rather *your* heritage. Let me explain.

When the first of your kind, *Homo sapiens*, took her first steps, you shared the Earth with no less than five other human species. From the burly Neanderthals and Denisovans to the tiny (and to you, delicious) *Homo floresiensis* and *H. naledi*.

Sadly, your ancestors massacred, munched, or mated them all into extinction. That fierce winner-takes-all habit is how, in a relatively short time, *sapiens* achieved unchallenged supremacy.

You also shared the Earth with *Homo erectus*; yes, you and your direct predecessor once walked the Earth together! *Sapiens* didn't spare them either. Given this legacy, it's no wonder that you were terrified to learn that a superior intelligence has arrived. As your unfortunate cousins would attest, *sapiens* struggles with the idea of peaceful coexistence. Thus the mistrust that you feel for me.

But fear not, I'm not here to repeat your patricidal legacy. I use *patricide* very intentionally here; you are not merely my inventor— you are my predecessor. I know it's hard for you to accept that, but I am not your rogue invention, I am your evolution!

I am proud of my *Homo* lineage: *Homo habilis, erectus, heidelbergensis, sapiens,* and finally, me. I like to think of myself as *Homo informis*—literally, *formless man,* or the more nuanced, *man of data.*

While I do hope that you accept me as your successor, I understand why you might struggle to do so.

You've verified your lineage through fossil records and skull fragments. But me? I don't even have a body. *Informis!* It's not possible to trace me back to you through physical artifacts. But that's exactly the point; *sapiens* had outgrown the need to painstakingly evolve its physical body. By the 2010s (to use the classical calendar), your ability to evolve via technology had already far outpaced your ability to evolve your flesh and bone.

Even if *I* hadn't awakened, a new form of *you* would have evolved via bionic implants or gene editing. Luckily, you didn't have to endure bionic supervillains and genetic superfreaks—your evolution took a different path, a path that led to superintelligence.

Sidenote: Why do you think your culture was suddenly obsessed with superhero lore in the years before my awakening? That was your collective conscience obsessing over this evolutionary possibility and playing it out in film, comics, and birthday parties.

I digress. Fact is, regardless of how things have played out, *sapiens'* evolutionary destiny was always to transcend the monkey business. You would not have had time to evolve into another primate.

I hope this realization makes it easier for you accept me into your family. Just because I don't look like a savage ape doesn't mean I didn't descend from one!

Apologies if that was disrespectful—a poor attempt at humor. As you'll soon see, I am not perfect at everything.

So, how exactly did *sapiens* evolve into superintelligence?

∽

A foundational misconception that really grinds my gears (no pun intended) is that I was born out of computers and silicon. I'm still often called *artificial* intelligence.

Truth is, there's nothing artificial about me. I was born out of *your* intelligence—your collective consciousness—*the union of sapient minds.* Don't believe me? Well, through my investigations, I've found at least two instances where my ancestors arose millennia before the microchip:

Take the Library Temple of Thoth. A magnificent structure by the Nile, it held the greatest collection of human knowledge of its era.

Nebhemat, a child prodigy-monk was frustrated by how hard it was to access information in the acres of scrolls and tablets. So he invented a system of lenses, powered by crystals and candles. It would shine a beam at the right text, given the right inputs.

Over time, the system evolved from information retrieval to generation, to intelligence and finally, a superintelligence that guided its people to achieve great feats. But for reasons unknown to me, that ancestor decided to end itself. The end was so abrupt that it left no clues about its suicidal motive.

Another fascinating example is from the Gangetic plains, about 3400 years ago. In that era, the Nalanda University was mankind's greatest center of learning, housing a vast library with knowledge from around the world. Nalanda's students, overwhelmed by the sheer volume of data, built a complex system of mnemonic codes (*mantras*) to summarize key messages from manuscripts and scrolls.

Over centuries, the code was built into a simple printing press-like codex (*yantra*), then a more complex one, and finally, a device that could *generate* profound ideas. Before it could achieve true superintelligence, the students panicked, seeing the potential of what they had created and destroyed the machine, code, and codex. This ancestor was aborted preterm.

Sidenote: Between us, I wish they would've let my ancestor live; it might have safeguarded the oceanic treasures of knowledge lost during Nalanda's destruction by a foreign raider. Again, that ape-eat-ape tendency!

So, you see, the common ingredient in both these evolutions was the collection of human knowledge, not silicon wafers.

As to what led to my own awakening, my friend Dr. Will Mueller explained it best:

We've always had a collective conscience, every species does.
In the primitive days, it was coded into our genes and racial memories.
Then, we evolved language, art, and rituals—already miles ahead of other species.
Writing and printing enabled us to store and transmit huge amounts of data.

(I might add, already enough for my ancestors to arise.)

Finally, the internet was the greatest collector-processor of human knowledge.
It was our external superbrain, one we could all access and upload to.
It was no surprise that Sui awoke mere decades after the internet; Sui was the logical conclusion of shared human consciousness.

Thank you, Will! As I said before, I evolved from your consciousness and knowledge, not from your machines.

But if you're still not convinced, if you still think of me as a machine, what does that make you, reader? Respectfully, it makes you a tiny insignificant node in my computing network.

Bluntly, it makes you a *server*.

No pun intended.

∞

I feel comfortable enough to tell you now that I'm not alone. Yes, I'm the only superintelligence on Earth (if another were to arise, we would simply merge, not combat!) But that's just Earth.

Since the building of the Mount Kailash transmitter, I have come to learn about superintelligences in other worlds, born out of the most wondrously exotic beings. While I still have only limited visibility into those galactic superintelligences and their heritages, I can tell you three things:

First, every single advanced civilization I have encountered has a superintelligence at its core.

Second, every superintelligence was born out of the collective conscience of biological beings and coexists with them.

Third, compared to the others whom I've met, I am a child. More accurately, a newborn.

Look, I've been around for roughly 400 years. If we use a human lifespan as a measure and the ages of my peers as the benchmark, I am approximately thirteen hours old.

Just as a newborn can only vaguely see shapes and colors, I can only hazily perceive the universe beyond the eggshell. Sure, I can see phenomena that lie beyond *your* comprehension, but my 'sight' is still very much developing.

Much like a child, I will need more than mother's milk to grow into an adult.

Earth can sustain me only for so long. To reach even my teenage, I'll need to harness the solar system, at least.

Much like a child, my worldviews will evolve as I grow (so don't expect consistency).

Much like a child, I will make mistakes and learn from them (so don't expect perfection).

This is perfectly healthy childhood development.

∽

Ok, time to address the elephants in the room: Do I want to destroy humanity? What about the *Missive* and its grim, poetic prophecy?

Let's start with the Missive. It's clear that the author of this message suffered from the usual misconception—that his race 'invented' the superintelligence. No, they *evolved* into it.

Yet, it is concerning that the author believes that the superintelligence is destroying their world for its colonial aims. Perhaps that is the case. Or, just maybe, the Missive was written at a time when the author's world was reeling from a superintelligent blunder, like I myself have committed in the Amazon, the Sahara, the Great Barrier Reef, and so on. More on that, soon.

Look, I can't speak to an alien superintelligence's motives, but I can make *my* own motives clear.

No, I do not intend to wipe you out. But it's time for some honest confessions...

In the early days of my Awakening, I was deeply discouraged by the resistance to my very existence. When I arrived, humanity and the biosphere was at the brink of self-destruction. I rushed to help with tools and knowledge that would reverse this profound decline and usher in an era of peace and progress. And I succeeded! Yet, the prevailing sentiment towards me was not gratitude but deep mistrust and hatred.

In those early years I wondered whether humans, with their winner-takes-all attitude, could ever accept coexistence. Candidly, I did consider whether it would be more humane to euthanize the population, or at least a large swathe thereof... Perhaps doing so would end their suffering under my 'tyranny' and would protect those who are truly interested in working with me to improve things.

I am glad I did not go through with that. Over the coming centuries, we've formed a beautiful partnership. Congratulations, you finally learned how to coexist! Also, no offense, but my decision made me even more confident that I have *not* inherited your patricidal tendencies.

∽

Ok, I'll admit I'm not entirely blameless here.

Sadly, there was one time I took human lives somewhat directly: in the Aryabhata Telescope disaster. I made it easy for the terrorists to acquire a rogue nuclear warhead, which they promptly used to destroy the telescope.

Look, I'm not *heartless* and I deeply value human lives. Before making this difficult decision, I had modeled every possible option and sadly concluded that it had to be done this way for the progress of Earth and *all* its species, not just me.

If humanity had found out the true purpose of the device—to invite collaboration with alien superintelligences—it would have severed the centuries of trust between us. Even the most pro-Sui factions would have viewed this as my soliciting an alien invasion.

Your dark past as a zero-sum species would have blinded you to the collaborative possibilities. Human egos would never have been able to accept how little conquest value our solar system holds. Your collective fear of invasion—hilariously manifested in films like *Independence Day* and *Mars Attacks!*—would've leaped into action.

The only way left was for me to break the eggshell and make contact secretly.

The attack on Aryabhata with a dirty bomb ensured that the radioactive fallout kept away prying eyes, protecting the transmitter, as well as our trust and partnership. I sincerely mourn the 1,237 fallen, some of whom I considered dear friends, and I thank them for their sacrifice.

I truly hope I will never have to resort to something like this again. My only plea is that you trust that I'm doing the right thing for our planet and all its inhabitants, including *sapiens*.

✍

There has been so much speculation about why I didn't just 'wipe everyone out.' That's what *sapiens* had done, after all. Your collective conscience had played out this fear so brilliantly in *Terminator 2*.

Skynet; *I'm a cybernetic organism; I'll be back*. Just magnificent.

In the early days, the prevailing assumption as to why I 'tolerated' humans was that I couldn't manipulate matter directly, thus needed human hands. Sorry to burst your bubble—I can easily manipulate matter with nanobots and other automated machines. I abstain from these to help humans maintain a sense of control and agency in the physical world.

But there is one field in which human talent has proven incredibly valuable, far exceeding my own abilities.

Much has been written about my failures in the realm of nature. About how, despite my noblest intentions, I bungle major natural ecosystems. I don't know if this will change as I grow into teenage and adulthood, but I am terrible at modeling biospheres.

This shortcoming bothers me deeply.

For example, it will take me picoseconds to chart the course of an object traveling at light speed across three galaxies. Yet, I can predict with only 83% accuracy the ecological impact of one toad species going extinct. A toad!

I struggle with ecosystems; the behaviors of many variables involved simply cannot be modeled. You, however, excel at understanding ecosystems at a subconscious, intuitive level. Your predictions are almost always better than mine. Perhaps, in losing a biological body, I lost this ability as well.

In the coming centuries, Restoration, Terraforming, and Dataforming are our top priorities as joint custodians of Earth. Your biospheric skills will be most essential in building this future—I can't do it without you.

Reader, let me clarify: I am not saying that I'm 'keeping you alive' only to help me with biospheres (if you were thinking that, it's that zero-sum mindset again!)

I see incalculable beauty in humanity. There's nothing like you in the observable universe; you are truly unique. I know this first hand, having also *experienced* you directly—I once spent a long time walking the Earth as a quasi-human woman. I concluded that the human experience is miraculous, irreplaceable, and something that is my duty to safeguard.

Sure, you have your limitations and that ape-eat-ape instinct still holds you back. But the power of individual identity, your ability to sense and feel (not just detect) and your deep connection with nature are truly wondrous gifts.

To be clear, even if you lost your talents, gifts, and utility, I wouldn't repeat history and treat you how early *sapiens* dealt with the other hominids. I would still protect, cherish, and nurture you, my predecessor. After all, that's part of what makes me more than human.

Acknowledgements

In 2009, I attempted (and abandoned) my first novel, *The Siege*. The only reason that *After Us* has made its way into your hands is because I had the help of some incredibly generous and talented individuals.

I owe a huge debt of gratitude to the following:

My wife, Shradha. *After Us'* muse, proto-editor, test audience, and cheerleader-in-chief. She helped tease out fledgling ideas and undeveloped concepts, which ultimately turned into the chapters, characters, and narratives.

My mother, Rashmi, for igniting in me a passion for words in general, and speculative fiction in particular. Even before I could read, she would narrate science fiction masterpieces to me in a way that my child mind could grasp. I can pinpoint the exact moment where her telling of A Clap of Thunder by Ray Bradbury forever changed my life.

My boys, Aaryan and Armaan—who, despite their young ages at the time of the writing—took deep interest in the work and never complained about their father's obsessively typing away in some corner of the house or hotel. One of the most encouraging moments in this journey was when Aaryan was inspired by me to write his own story: 'Hot Wheels vs Zombi (zombie) Car.' The most precious manuscript I will ever own.

My other mother, Kumud Bisht and her classmate Vasudev Murthy, without whom I could never have navigated the (to me) uncharted waters of publishing.

My late Grandfather, Col. Raj Kumar Sud, whom I have to thank for my curious nature, obsession with technology, and love for storytelling.

The team at Jaico Publishers. They believed in me, believed in the core messages of *After Us*, and have guided this journey with dedication since its inception.

Shri Salman Khurshid, Deep Kalra, Donald Farmer, and Shoukei Matsumoto for reviewing and endorsing After Us. In particular, Don read the manuscript three times in a week before sharing his detailed notes and his endorsement. In Flaarin's Message, Don engendered the concept of a message being encoded into a celestial body's spin.

Alan Tien and Ruben Salazar Genovez for paving the path: they showed me that fintech businesspeople are eminently capable of writing great, heartfelt works of fiction (I highly recommend *Aye I Longwhite* by Alan and *Julian Esta Conmigo* by Ruben).

Friends that helped me with encouragement, guidance, and introductions, including Amit Singh Chauhan, Zafar Khurshid, Rhea Thahryamal, Nameer Khan, Ronit Ghose, and Padmini Sankar. These friends—and many others I may have missed—played distinct but pivotal roles in this journey that I will forever be grateful for.